The Actor
Who Laughed

The Actor Who Laughed

FRANK THRING & ROLAND ROCCHECCIOLI

Illustrated by VANE LINDESAY

Hutchinson of Australia

HUTCHINSON GROUP (Australia) Pty Ltd
16–22 Church Street, Hawthorn, Victoria, 3122

Melbourne Sydney London
Auckland Johannesburg
and agencies throughout the world

First published 1985
© Frank Thring & Roland Rocchecioli 1985
Typeset by ProComp Productions Pty Ltd, South Australia
Printed and bound by Globe Press Pty Ltd, Victoria

All rights reserved. No part of this publication
may be reproduced, stored in a retrieval system, or
transmitted, in any form or by any means, electronic,
mechanical, photocopying, recording or otherwise,
without the prior permission of the Publisher.

National Library of Australia
Cataloguing in Publication Data:
Thring, Frank, 1926– .
 The actor who laughed.
 ISBN 0 09 137860 5.
 1. Actors — Anecdotes, facetiae, satire, etc.
 2. Moving-picture actors and actresses — Anecdotes,
 facetiae, satire, etc. I. Rocchecioli, Roland. II. Title.
792'.028'0922

Foreword

It gives me great pleasure to write a Foreword to this book, *The Actor Who Laughed*. I have found it most amusing, interesting and informative.

It was so nice to read a book about the theatre in which it is quite clear that actors can be amusing, funny and entertaining. I have always found it so and find it marvellous to be able to have a record of such things.

I congratulate the authors on being clever in collecting such amusing material.

Sir Robert Helpmann CBE

Acknowledgements

Christine Amor, Andrew Barker, Rosemary Barr, Kenn Brodziak OBE, June Bronhill MBE, Joan Bruce, Barbara Cartland D. St. J., Gordon Chater, Liddy Clarke, James Coburn, Peter Collingwood, Eileen Colocott, Hugh Colman, Malcolm Cooke, Ian Cookesley, Ruth Cracknell AM, Angie Dickinson, David Downer, Betty Druitt, Noel Ferrier, Alan Finney, Rodney Fisher, Margaret Ford MBE, John Frost, Betty Gooday, Sandy Gore, Ken Gregory, Maureen Hafner, Jennifer Hagan, Nancye Hayes, Sir Robert Helpmann CBE, John Michael Howson, Brian James, John McCallum CBE, Edgar Metcalfe, Harry M. Miller, Helen Montague, Wilton Morley, Patti Mostyn, Bruce Myles, John Orcsik, Robert Parsons, Johnny Quinn, Debbie Reynolds, Peter Salmon, John Stanton, John Sumner CBE, Berys Underhill, Garry Van Egmond, Stuart Wagstaff, Jennifer West, Googie Withers AO.

A Word from the Authors

I hope that in the writing of these anecdotes I have not offended anyone. Certainly I have not meant to cause any unhappiness, only to share the great pleasure I have derived from my profession. I hope the famous—and the infamous—who are mentioned in these stories are blessed with the same sense of humour as myself, something which I regard as absolutely essential to survive in this crazy business.

I would ask all who are about to read this book to think on the closing speech from *A Midsummer Night's Dream*—it says it all!

> If we shadows have offended,
> Think but this, and all is mended,
> That you have but slumber'd here
> While these visions did appear.
> And this weak and idle theme,
> No more yielding but a dream,
> Gentles, do not reprehend:
> If you pardon, we will mend,
> And, as I am an honest Puck,
> If we have unearned luck
> Now to scape the Serpent's tongue,
> We will make amends ere long;
> Else the Puck a liar call:
> So, good night unto you all.
> Give me your hands, if we be friends,
> And Robin shall restore amends.

Roland Roccheccioli

I hope that in the writing of these anecdotes I *have* offended someone, otherwise the sales will be non-existent.

Not sharing Roland's roseate view of the profession, I was

delighted to find my more jaundiced outlook shared by no less a practitioner of the art than Miss Glenda Jackson, whom I quote from a recent newspaper interview:

> It's not a life that I like. I find it deeply unnatural to go to work when most people are coming home. The physical conditions are usually painful and unpleasant and cold and draughty. Why do it? The only reason for doing it is the work itself, and if that doesn't have some quality, forget it. Every time you start something it's as if you've never acted in your life before. You have to find it in you every time. What's been done is no guarantee that you'll be able to do it again. The minute I say 'Yes, I'll do it', I think 'Christ, I can't. I don't know *how* to do it.'

So now you know that when actors laugh, it is not humour but hysteria.

I would ask all who are about to read this book to think on Shakespeare's most famous stage direction, 'Exit— pursued by a bear'— it says it all!

Frank Thring

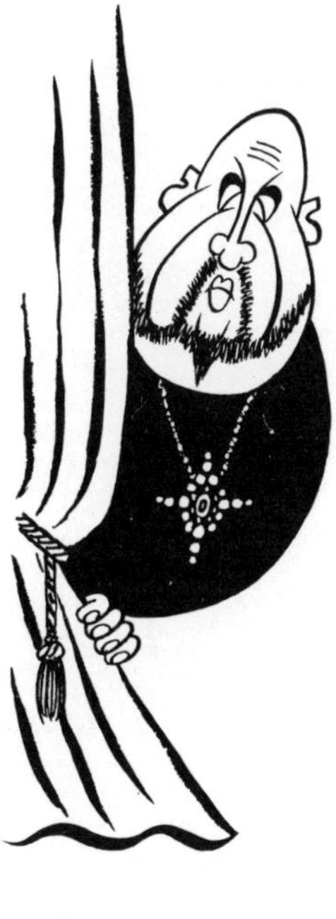

Let us start where we all finish, at death's door. This ill-lit exit is, after all, the only one beyond which an actor cannot take his ego. When John Barrymore, afloat in absinthe and ammonia, cirrhosis triumphant, and unable to read the lines let alone remember them, noticed that his friends were slightly perturbed, he waved them away with a liver-spotted hand and said, 'Don't worry, don't worry. Barrymores never die. That is for commoners.'

Having been dragged from theatre to theatre and from bar to bar since he was a child he had developed an unquenchable thirst for the hard stuff by the time he was fourteen. He was, however, possessed of such physical beauty and charm that half the English-speaking world seemed to devote their lives to protecting him from himself. Frank Case, controller of the Algonquin, then, as now, the only hotel in New York, saw Barrymore appear in the restaurant at what was, for him, a remarkably early hour—perhaps 11 a.m. 'Breakfast', cried Barrymore, summoning a minion. When the waiter arrived with a menu, Barrymore waved it aside and said, 'Create for me an absinthe frappé. On second thoughts, and I always have second thoughts when I am dying, create two.' Case signalled the waiter to take his time with the drinks and said to Barrymore, 'Come and have a cup of coffee with me while you're waiting'. Barrymore consumed endless cups of coffee and when Case conveyed to the staff that it was time to bring on the absinthe, Barrymore didn't even bother to drink it.

Several days later Barrymore seized Case as he was passing through the hotel lobby and cried, 'Jesus, that was a great idea of yours, Frank. Brilliant, absolutely brilliant.' Taken aback, Case looked at the Great Profile and queried, 'What? What's so great?' Barrymore hugged him close and said wonderingly, 'Only you could have thought of it. *Coffee. Coffee* for *breakfast!*'

Whilst digging his grave with a corkscrew, Barrymore had ample time to watch many of his friends pursue their own way to dusty death. One of these was Sadakichi, whose occupation nowadays would be listed as 'Guru'. Half German and half Japanese, Sadakichi had been brought to a mutual friend's house after being found near to death from a haemorrhage in the shack he inhabited on a convenient Indian reservation. What a German-Japanese was doing on an Indian reservation has been lost in the alcoholic fumes of Barrymore's memory. He does recall, though, that when he arrived Sadakichi was berating the company for not having obtained a coffin in preparation for his imminent death.

Barrymore was outraged. 'Have you any proper defence', he orated, 'for refusing this amiable and practical request for a sarcophagus?'

It was explained to Barrymore that there was some local ruling that a coffin bought at wholesale by a layman could not be accepted for burial. This obvious sop to the money-grabbing morticians threw Barrymore into a frenzy of rage.

'Sadakichi is not a layman', he stormed, 'Look! Look there.' A snake-like arm pointed to the parchment-skinned skeleton barely breathing in a sagging hammock.

'I invite you to glance at him dying there and then look me in the eye and dare to tell me that his dying is not the work of a *great professional!*'

While both were staggering around Hollywood, trying to stand up straight in front of the cameras and read cue cards simultaneously, John Barrymore, the great actor, and W. C. Fields, the great comedian, expressed their views on the Demon Rum in characteristically different ways. Barrymore, only a few flagons away from death, said, 'Don't let anyone tell you that you can drown yourself in drink. You can't. I've tried. You float.'

Mr Fields, who had a penchant for gin because he could always pretend it was a glass of water, was asked by a foolhardy reporter why he didn't actually drink water. 'Water?' snorted Fields. 'Water? Filthy stuff. Fishes f_____ in it!'

Harry Cohn, the head of Columbia Pictures when they actually made pictures, will be remembered not for the Hitlerian manner in which he ran the company ('I don't get ulcers', he screamed at some grovelling secretary, '*I give them*') but rather for his unofficial epitaph which was spoken by Red Skelton on his television show the night of Cohn's funeral. 'I was at Harry Cohn's funeral service today', said Skelton in his best graveside manner, 'and I was just stunned by the thousands and thousands of people who were there. Gee, it only proves what Harry often said . . . people will always come out for what they want to see.'

On the other hand, Louis B. Mayer's funeral was strangely ill-attended. While the Hollywood hacks were discussing this amongst themselves, Sam Goldwyn's voice cut through the waffle. 'Forget it', he said. 'Forget it. These people have come here like I have . . . to make sure he's dead.'

I was comfortably ensconced in my railway carriage en route to Venice or somewhere, when Laurence Olivier charged in and sank glowering in the otherwise empty compartment.

'Thank God you're here', he said. 'I've just had the most dreadful experience.'

Reaching for the brandy, as I have been through a few dreadful experiences with him before, I asked what particularly dreadful experience he had just had.

'I've just done Winston Churchill's obituary for the BBC.'
'But he isn't dead', I said.
'That's the point, you fool', snarled Larry, snatching the

brandy from me in a gesture that was reminiscent of his seizing the crown in *Richard III*. 'Don't you realize that the BBC keep thousands of these things on tape waiting for people to die so that they can go on air in five minutes and cover everything—tapes, video, the lot?'

The glass was thrust back into my hand for a refill. I filled it and, after having a quick swig, handed it back. Knowing how much Larry admired Churchill (he had based his performance as Titus Andronicus on him), I started my soothing routine . . . 'Now Larry, I know how much Winston means to you. Do you remember how nervous you were when he came to see *Titus* and you thought he might think that you were getting a bit too close in your interpretation? Churchill would be delighted if he knew that you were doing his obituary—he probably asked for you. What are you so worried about?'

The basilisk eyes turned on me like a torch. 'Are you mad?' he demanded. 'Thousands of obituaries in the archives . . . I've just done Churchill's . . . who's going to do *mine*?'

Actors and actresses are obsessed with age and its concomitant, death. Dietrich, making one of her innumerable (but not unfortunately endless) farewell appearances, insisted that the publicity photographs be taken by an artist of the camera whose work had pleased her exacting standards some fifteen years before. When confronted by the results she expressed her disapproval.

'You must forgive me', said the world famous photographer, 'but you must remember that I am fifteen years older'.

For all those artists who spent their butterfly lives concealing their age instead of revealing their talent, Dorothy Parker, as usual, had the last word. Dedicating it to an unnamed actress, Miss Parker penned this epitaph:

> Her name cut clear upon this marble cross,
> Shines, as it shone when she was still on earth;
> While tenderly the mild agreeable moss
> Obscures the figures of her date of birth.

For one reason or another actors are still looked upon as rogues and vagabonds despite the plethora of lords and knights who besprinkle the profession like jewels upon an old costume. While this may be due to the unnatural preoccupation that the world's media have with them, it must be admitted that actors do have a predilection for both physical and verbal self-destruction. Able to rush upon a stage and shout their way through anything from *King Lear* to *Charley's Aunt*, they usually find themselves incapable of skimming through even the simplest shallows of everyday life.

Richard Burton, uncharacteristically sober and attending one of those chi-chi social occasions that he avoided like syphilis, found himself seated between the Queen Mother and Princess Margaret. Having had an enchanting time talking to the Queen Mother he turned, at an appropriate moment, to the formidable Meg. 'Ah', he said, 'I was just talking to your . . . er . . . um . . . er . . .'

Princess Margaret stabbed him with the steely stare that had sunk a thousand serfs. 'I believe the phrase you're searching for is "Her Majesty, The Queen Mother".' The rest of the meal was not exactly fun-time.

Burton seems to have been particularly accident-prone when it came to the occasional *faux-pas*. As a young actor he was partial to imitating the great stars of the time, positions that most of them still maintain. Having worked his way through Olivier, Richardson, *et al*, he had just launched into his impersonation of Sir John Gielgud when he became aware of an unseasonable frost descending on his audience. He turned to find Sir John standing watching him with a keen interest.

After one of his famous pauses and in the dulcet tones for which he is renowned, Sir John said, 'My dear boy, generally speaking, very good impersonators do not make very good actors'.

When we were touring Europe with the triumphant Olivier *Titus Andronicus*, Larry responded to the standing ovations with a little speech in the language of the country in which we happened to be playing. This worked well enough in Paris and Venice, but became a bit stickier in Vienna, and bogged down completely in Belgrade, Zagreb and Warsaw. Larry's solution appeared to be simplicity itself. As we were greeted everywhere by Embassy officials and troupes of translators Larry would immediately hand in his brief thank-you speech, have it changed into the appropriate tongue, go through it, write it out phonetically, and learn it. In the more exotic countries, this touching gesture was received with rapturous cries and even more stamping and applause. Until, that is, the first night in Warsaw where the audience, packed with Commissars of the Arts, the Ministry of Culture and half the top brass of the Red Army, were startled to hear the great Olivier tell them in perfect Polish, hand on heart and voice quivering with sincerity, 'You are our last stop in Europe. We have travelled many miles to get here and now we all want to f_____ you.'

Judging by the reaction, one got the impression that they were rather taken with the idea. They screamed with delight and laughter for some time until Larry, completely nonplussed at the result of his words, finally joined the rest of the company and, amongst much waving, smiles, and hisses of 'mad Poles', the curtain fell. In a flash the interpreters, hysterical with mirth, were running amongst us pointing out that in Polish the pronunciation of the magic word differed but infinitesimally from the word 'thank'. Larry never got it wrong again, but for the rest of the season seventy actors suddenly fell about when he reached a certain spot in his curtain speech.

Surprised though they may have been by Olivier's proposition, at least the audience was good-humoured about it. It was not always thus however. Macready once had half the carcase of a freshly-killed sheep slung at him from the gallery. John Barrymore, on the other hand, reversed this procedure when he became so enraged at the storm of coughing roaring through the audience that he suddenly threw a large fish at them and cried, 'Busy yourselves with that, you damned walruses, and let us get on with the play'.

Barrymore got his come-uppance on a similar occasion when one single hacking cougher was disrupting his famous *Hamlet*. Having spotted the offender, Barrymore kept flashing demonic glances at him during speech after speech. The coughing continued unabated. Barrymore, livid with rage, walked down to the footlights and, hands on hips, stared in thunderous silence at the man for an eternity. A hush fell over the house to be broken only when the cougher slowly rose to his feet and, as quietly as possible, dragged himself along the row, up the centre aisle and out of the theatre ... on crutches.

When, towards the end of the seventeenth century, women were beginning to take over the parts played by 'pretty men and boys' the risk of on-stage disaster became even greater. At a performance of *King Lear*, the great David Garrick was lying with his head in the lap of Peg Woffington, who was playing Cordelia, when one of the audience leapt onto the stage and, in the words of an eye-witness, 'assaulted her with the utmost indecency'. Garrick apparently ignored the whole thing because he knew that if he intervened he would be skewered by the patron's sword. In those days audiences knew how to keep actors in their places.

Talking of sexual assault, the trigger for the unlikely plot of the aforementioned *Titus Andronicus* was the rape and mutilation of Titus's daughter, Lavinia. Vivien Leigh took the part, rather unselfishly I thought, as after being gang-banged in the first half-hour of the play, she suffered several other indignities. Her assailants (who were friends of the family) tore out her tongue and cut off her hands, leaving her to wander around the stage for the rest of the night with her stumps bound in white gauze discreetly streamered with blood. Eventually it occurs to her that she could write the names of the rapists in the earth. Gingerly she takes a staff from one of her entourage and, holding it between the handless arms, painstakingly proceeds to spell out the names. At one performance the staff slipped from her feeble grasp and, watched by an appalled cast, rolled down the stage and over the edge into the front row.

Whilst the cream of the Stratford Company considered who was going to retrieve it, a woman in the front row hesitantly picked it up and laid it on the stage. Still, given her handless condition, Vivien could not pick it up. At least ten actors eventually made a dive for it. It was snatched up by Olivier, returned to Vivien, and the play proceeded on its merry way.

Afterwards Noel Coward, who had watched the whole debacle with tears running down his face, poked his head round Vivien's dressing-room door. 'Butter-stumps', he cried merrily and darted out again.

For this tale we are indebted to Gene Fowler, wit, author, and drinking companion of Barrymore. The actor-manager William Collier was one of the first to give the young Barrymore a job, largely because of the established reputations of brother Lionel and sister Ethel. After a successful American season, the play *The Dictator* crossed the Atlantic for presentation in London. On the opening night, two of Mr Collier's actors put him in a fine

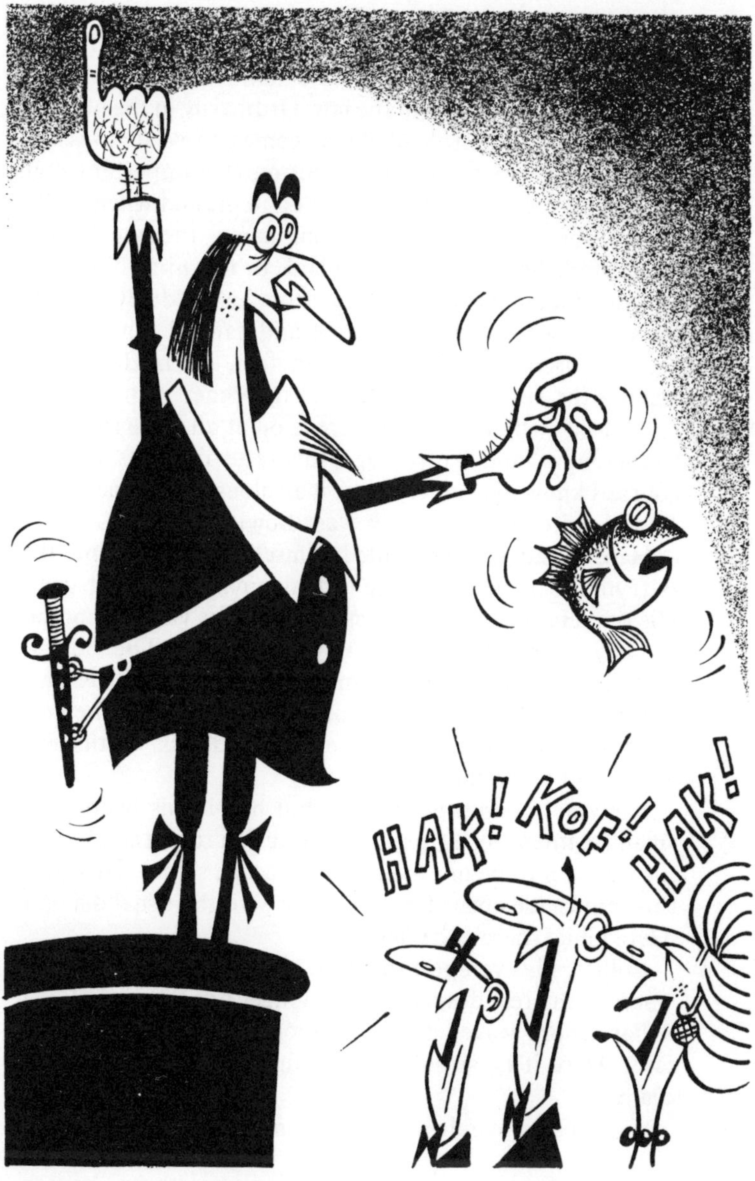
HAK! KOF! HAK!

predicament. Barrymore, of course, was the worst offender. At the rise of the curtain on *The Dictator*, Collier, as Travers, is found in desperate need of a new name to cover his identity as a fugitive from the law. Ordinarily in the play, one of his actors in the role of Bowie comes on-scene to sell his name to Travers for $25,000. But on this important night the actor appeared with alcoholic hauteur, and when Collier asked, 'By the way, what is your name, the one I am to purchase?', he refused point-blank to tell him. Nor could Collier squeeze the name 'Bowie' from his suddenly obstinate actor. He wheedled, threatened and cajoled him, but the actor refused all information. In fact, he made an exit, leaving the first-nighters in total ignorance of his identity or, indeed, why he had ever come on at all. The marooned Collier, alone and centre stage, finally ad-libbed, saying, 'Of course I know his name. Knew it all along. Happened to run into his wife. She told me it was "Bowie".'

Hardly had Collier hauled himself out of this pit than Barrymore arrived on-stage to make matters far, far worse. His first entrance as a wireless operator was vitally important for any proper understanding of the play. The business provided that Barrymore hand Collier a wireless despatch written on two long sheets of paper. Collier would then read the report aloud, thus advising the audience of the why, when, and wherefore of the plot.

Barrymore appeared on cue, but had in his hand only a small fragment torn from a menu card, a tiny triangle about the size of a Cape of Good Hope postage stamp. He offered this minuscule absurdity to Collier with the usual dialogue, 'Here Chief, here's the despatch'.

Collier, his eye upon the wisp of paper, improvised, 'But where is the real despatch? The longer one?'

Barrymore waved the microscopic message at him and said, 'Here it is, sir. Or have your eyes gone back on you again?'

'Go to the wireless room', commanded the desperate

Collier, 'and bring the *first* despatch. There are two sheets of it. Remember? That's the one I want to read. Not a piece of confetti.'

'But this *is* the first despatch', Barrymore insisted, 'I took it down myself, word for word'.

Collier knew that the long plot-point speech that he was supposed to deliver could never be accepted by the audience as having been written on this menu fragment. 'Get the prop', he hissed, 'or I'll break your leg'. Then, so that the audience could hear, he said, 'Someone is trying to double-cross us. Go back and look again. I'm sure you'll find the genuine message.'

'But I know this is the genuine message, sir', Barrymore persisted. 'It was sent by a well-known female impersonator.'

'Then have her, or him, send us another one.'

'But', Barrymore said, 'he, or she, can't. He, or it, just died. Are you going to the funeral?'

'No', said Collier. 'How can I?'

'Why not, sir?'

'Because', screamed the frenzied Collier, 'I haven't got a black dress!' Sotto voice he whispered, 'It's a terrible thing to be stranded in London. Get it?' Aloud he said, 'Now go for the other message'.

Barrymore saluted and went off-stage, leaving the tottering star to ad-lib once again for almost half a minute. Then Barrymore re-appeared to present him with exactly the same triangular piece of paper.

'Sir, I have just had this authenticated', he said and he held up the pathetic little scrap. 'It was not written by the late female impersonator, but by that very clever fellow who engraves the Lord's Prayer on the heads of pins'.

There was no other course for the exhausted Collier, by this time a gibbering wreck, than to take the miserable paper, hurriedly edit down his regular speech and hope for the best. He had barely reached the close of his severely abridged reading when the actor who hitherto had refused to give the name 'Bowie' entered unexpectedly to shout, 'I've decided to tell you my name. It's John P. Murphy!'

The play ran for more than a year.

Not all actors' misfortunes befall them on the stage: the most innocuous social occasion can be as fraught with danger as a minefield.

When Laurence Olivier and Vivien Leigh were living in a minute house in Chelsea they decided to celebrate something (Larry's divorce . . . a new film . . . Guy Fawkes Day . . . who cares?) by inviting Ralph and Meriel Richardson to dinner. The house, although tiny, was furnished and decorated in Vivien's usual exquisite taste. Not a piece of fabric nor a painting had been installed without the scrutiny of her fabulous eyes.

To enhance the celebration (perhaps it *was* Guy Fawkes Day) the Richardsons had brought champagne and fireworks, both of which they all proceeded to enjoy in the handkerchief-sized, walled garden.

Suddenly, one of the Richardsons' more extravagant purchases took off like a rocket (which in fact it was), ricochetted round the mellow brick walls and shot through the French windows, burying itself in a delicate, mushroom-coloured velvet-covered Victorian sofa from whence it continued to send out a peacock's tail of multi-hued sparks as it burrowed its way into the pristine upholstery. Very soon afterwards the Richardsons disappeared into the night.

Some years later when the Oliviers, wedded, wealthy, and acclaimed, had purchased the breath-taking Notley Abbey, Vivien had calmed down sufficiently to allow the Richardsons to be invited for the weekend. The Abbey, founded in the twelfth century by the Augustine monks, had been visited by both Henry V and Cardinal Wolsey, a fact that endeared it to Larry and, indeed, he bought it with the money that he earned from his great *Henry V* film. Vivien went to work on a mammoth scale — panelling was restored,

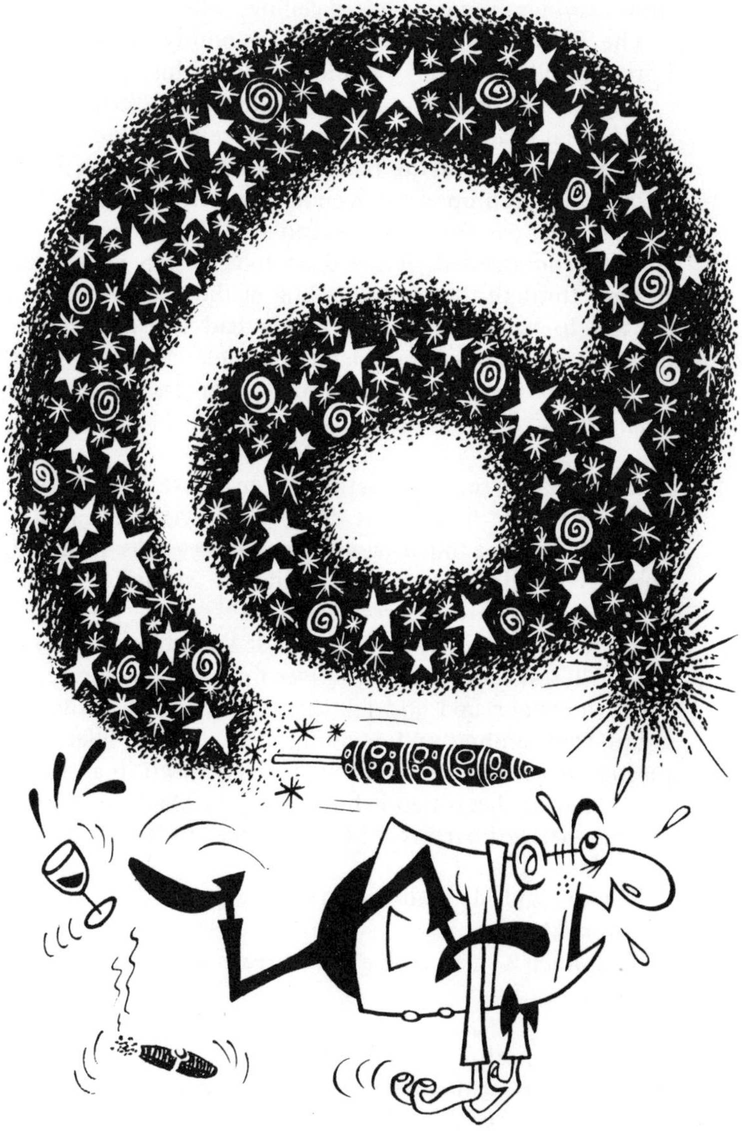

stone carvings cleaned, vaulted ceilings retouched with gilt.

The Richardson weekend went smoothly enough until Larry, extolling the joy of finding bits of history in every niche, insisted on taking Ralph up into the cavernous roof where great beams, hand-painted with religious motifs, had been discovered. Having reached the hallowed spot, Larry flashed his torch upon the wonders and cried, 'There, look at those. Get over there so you can see them properly.'

Thus commanded, Richardson took a step back, went straight through the plaster ceiling of the master-bedroom on which, not unnaturally, Vivien had lavished endless money, time and taste, and landed in a cloud of dust on the immense double bed. The Richardsons were last seen driving, at an excessive speed, up the road that led to London.

Miss June Allyson, the definitive girl next door, (if you happened to be living next door to MGM) is the first to admit that she is a touch vague on social occasions. Lunching one day in Hollywood, she noticed a stunning-looking woman sweep into the restaurant flanked by two equally jazzy men. When they were seated at the table next to her, Miss Allyson ventured a tentative smile. This was received with a gracious nod and for the rest of the meal the two ladies kept smiling and nodding at each other like those plastic ducks that keep bobbing up and down in a glass of water. At luncheon's end the woman, no doubt exhausted by this extraordinary charade, leant over to Baby June and said, 'Ann-Margret'.

'Oh no', said Miss Allyson, 'I'm very flattered but, no, I'm not Ann-Margret'.

The other woman took a deep breath and said, 'Not you . . . *me*'.

Miss Allyson also recounts another unfortunate mealtime debacle when, at the height of the Taylor-Fisher-Reynolds clash, she was dining with a circle which included Elizabeth T. and Eddie F. Try as she might Miss Allyson could not refrain from calling Liz 'Debbie'. After an hour of this, plus the subsequent embarrassed silences and mumbled apologies, Miss Taylor rested her bosom on the table and said very sweetly, 'Look, why don't you just call me "George".'

Invited to see Peter Brook's monumental (though slightly eccentric) production of Seneca's *Oedipus* starring Sir John Gielgud and Dame Irene Worth, Sir Ralph Richardson and his wife struck trouble before the play had even started: let him tell it.

'When I went to see the production, somehow I hadn't got a programme. So I said to my wife, "Leave it to me", and I went down the aisle to a chap, but he was lashed to a pillar. I didn't know what was going on. It turned out that he was in the show. I think he was one of the chorus. But the show hadn't started yet. My wife said, "Did you get a programme?" And I had to say it wasn't possible because all the programme sellers were lashed to the dress-circle. Very strange. And when I asked him for a programme all I got were these strangled sounds. The poor chappie was gagged, you see. The whole experience upset me very much. I'm a very square man.'

It was the same production that prompted one of Gielgud's more inspired *bon mots*. Dame Irene Worth, having discovered that she had absent-mindedly borne two children by her own son, was called upon to rush onto the stage and impale herself on a triangular, phallic spike. Came the magic moment at the first full rehearsal and on screamed the Dame to be confronted by a bronze spike perhaps twelve inches long. Having envisaged something the size of a Stonehenge column, Dame Irene was slightly taken aback.

'Is there something wrong dear?' called Peter Brook from the stalls.

'Well', said the Dame, 'I'd imagined something bigger—three or four feet—perhaps on a big plinth'.

'Who did you have in mind, dear?' asked Gielgud, who had been watching with his usual detached amusement, 'Plinth Philip or Plinth Charles?'

Peter Brook was notorious for his original, exciting and not infrequently infuriating methods of enticing performances from his casts, stars and extras alike. During rehearsals for an immense production of *The Tempest* at Drury Lane, he asked the cast (some fifty of them) to walk down to the edge of the stage and tell him and an empty auditorium the most dreadful thing that they could possibly think of.

One by one, bedraggled in work-clothes, pale and without make-up, they straggled down to the footlights and spoke of child-molestation, incest, crucifixion, cancer, sodomy and rape. There, on a bare stage, they exorcised their worst horrors before the all-healing director. Finally, cool and immaculate as always, Gielgud, who happened to be playing the immense leading part of Prospero, glided towards the vast, black space.

'John', called Brook, 'we've heard from everyone else. What is the most horrifying thing that you can imagine?'

Gielgud looked into the darkness and said, 'We open in three weeks'.

But let us join Googie Withers for a final *faux pas*. A gracious and charming hostess, she was taking a rather refined collection of friends to see a play that starred her old film-making confrère, Robert (Long John Silver) Newton. Robert, an alcoholic of Bacchanalian proportions, had been warned by Googie to be on his best behaviour when she brought her rarefied group backstage to meet him. Nevertheless, it was with some trepidation that she guided them into the dressing-room. All, miraculously, was well. Newton, dressing-gowned, charming and, to the uninitiated, sober, dispensed drinks and everybody mingled, chatting happily. Just as Googie was breathing a sigh of relief, the gay badinage faded except for Newton who continued telling an amusing anecdote to entertain his guests. Simultaneously he was peeing in the dressing-room basin.

For some reason that escapes me, actors and their ilk are supposed to be capable of dropping *bon mots* at the fall of a *chapeau*. Regardless of the situation, be it ladies luncheons, cocktail parties, or the dreaded television, radio and press interviews, it is invariably expected that we let flow a Niagara of wit to drown the incompetence of those incapable of amusing themselves.

The notorious airport press posse is a hideous example. Fortunately there are a valiant few who are capable of holding their own, even when confronted by this rapacious rabble.

Noel Coward, who was not called the Master for nothing, managed to cope in the face of their idiocies with his usual aplomb. Coward, having been whisked into the press room at Sydney Airport, tottering with jet-lag, was asked by some fool of a reporter, 'Mr Coward, it has been said that you are a homosexual; it this true?'

With a pitying look, Coward replied, 'Certainly not . . . but the gentleman I sleep with is'.

Still surrounded by the hyena hordes, he was attacked by yet another harpy who hadn't done her homework, this time from the *Sun* newspaper. 'Tell me', she shrilled across the clamorous hacks, 'have you anything to say to the *Sun*?'

'Certainly', said Noel, 'SHINE'.

Magnificent Martita Hunt, famous for her performance as Miss Haversham in *Great Expectations*, was staying at a Beverly Hills Hotel when a young reporter arrived to interview her. When he asked for her at the desk, the clerk said that he was expected but that Miss Hunt was rather odd.

'Odd', said the reporter, nose twitching like a beagle on the scent. 'What do you mean, odd?'

'Well', said the clerk, 'she never goes out. Meals, wardrobe fittings, everything has to be done in her suite'.

The reporter was sent up to Martita and opened the interview with, 'Miss Hunt, I understand that you never leave the suite, that everything is sent into you. Why do you never go out?'

'Go out', thundered Martita, who had a voice like a church organ, 'Go out! Are you mad? There are *Americans* out there.'

Of course, the actor has to cope with enemies other than the press, notably his fellow artists. Compared to the venom of his colleagues, the pusillanimous little boys of the press are as acid to arsenic. When, at the end of their first, and only, film together Katharine Hepburn said to John Barrymore, 'Thank Christ, I'll never have to act with you again', Barrymore crooned, 'I didn't know you ever had, darling'.

When Dame Edith Evans was teamed with Dame Sybil Thorndike in *Waters of the Moon*, a few dramas, other than those in the script, were to be expected. Sybil, playing the proprietress of a rather run-down country house which accepted paying guests, was confronted by a Rolls-Royce-transported, Balenciaga-clad, snow-bound Dame Edith Evans. Not unnaturally, a tiny tension arose between these two swingers, both in their seventies. Equally unsurprisingly, the play was an enormous success. After the first year, Dame Edith wandered into the management and said, 'Now darlings, the play has been running a long time. I think I should pop over to Paris and get a couple of new Balenciagas, perhaps half a dozen pairs of shoes, a couple of fresh fur coats, and some stockings and gloves.' She paused and said,

'Oh, and if this thing is going to run another year, you'd better get poor old Sybil another cardigan'.

During the course of the play it was required that Dame Sybil play a nostalgic something on the piano while Dame Edith, caught up in the gaiety, did a little waltz around the stage. Amused by this barrage of Balenciaga, Dame Sybil decided to play the piece a little faster and faster until Dame Edith, who had to keep time with the music, was incapable of getting out her lines. When they met in the dismal dressing-room corridors later, Dame Sybil smiled at Dame Edith and said, 'And I can play faster too'.

During rehearsals for this production there was a certain tension concerning the learning of lines; understandable considering that the six principals had notched up about five hundred years between them. One dull afternoon, the play ground slowly to a halt and the prompter's voice was heard in the land. The actors busied themselves with other things (knitting, lighting cigarettes, picking up books, blowing noses) while the hapless prompter rasped the line from offstage at an increasing pitch of hysteria.

When this had gone on for what Dame Edith considered a sufficient time she turned to the prompt corner and said, with camel-like hauteur, 'We know the line, dear boy, just tell us who says it'.

When George Cukor was directing *The Women* with an all-female cast, pyrotechnics were expected and, given the line-up (Norma Shearer, Joan Crawford, Joan Fontaine, Paulette Goddard and Rosalind Russell) they were not long in detonating. One of the key sequences took place in a chic couturier's, with Ros Russell subjecting Shearer to a stream of scandal while Norma was being fitted for a dress. Cukor wanted Russell in close-up, hissing her malice in Shearer's ear but, when the time came for a take, Miss Russell found it impossible to get near the lady, who had slipped into a crinoline, black and eight feet wide, successfully preventing anyone getting within speaking distance. Cukor, and Miss Russell, were not unequal to this unexpected challenge. Given a trice they arranged a three-way mirror in front of Miss Shearer and, adjusting the camera angle, Cukor crooned villainously, 'That's much better, Norma dear. Now there are four Rosalind Russells and only one of you.'

As Joan Fontaine and Olivia de Havilland will tell you (next time you're chatting to them), family ties build no barricades when it gets down to good old-fashioned bitchery, which it frequently does. When Zsa Zsa Gabor was out here to flitter through The Michael Parkinson Show, she was being shown around Sydney and suddenly felt deep down in her deep Hungarian soul that she needed a pizza to get her through the day. Waving aside the minions who were supposed to whisk her from engagement to engagement, she zipped into the nearest Pizza Hut where she caused as much excitement as a bird of paradise in a hen house.

Finally, the young man who had been attending to her order gathered himself together and said, 'Excuse me, aren't you Eva Gabor?' Clutching her pizza very tightly, *La Dame Sans Merci* twinkled at the poor thing and said, 'No, darlink . . . I am Zsa Zsa Gabor'. Then, seeing the young pizza-pusher's embarrassment, she added, 'But I look so dreadful to day, it's no wonder you think I'm Eva'.

Sir Noel Coward, hounded out of England by the crucifying taxes, burrowed away at a place in Jamaica or thereabouts and when asked why he had chosen that particular plot said, 'The natives are very sweet; they spend their entire time indulging in what can only be described as sexual intercourse with a winsome disregard for gender'.

When, ill unto death, unable to eat, he was asked what he would say to a little fish for breakfast he said, 'I'd say "Hello, little fish".' Though not a death-bed line, it ranks with Oscar Wilde who, dying in a Parisian slum, looked around him and said, 'I knew when I saw that wallpaper, that one of us would have to go'.

Mr Stuart Wagstaff, the eminent star of stage, screen, and you name it, is responsible for some of the more scurrilous stories in this slim volume and he has just fired another barrage of bitchery from his formidable arsenal of anecdotes.

The larger than life Tallulah Bankhead, inexplicably invited to the wedding of two mutual friends, was remarkably restrained during the long, interminable ceremony. However, at the magic moment when veils were being lifted and kisses exchanged, the rasping Bankhead baritone reverberated through the church. 'I don't know why they bother. They're both lousy in bed.'

On one occasion when she was seated alongside an actress whose main claim to fame was that she had climbed the rungs of the Hollywood ladder without losing her virginity, Bankhead remained ominously silent until one of the other ladies present asked, 'Is it true darling, are you still a virgin?'

'Oh yes', simpered the actress, 'I still have my cherry'.

'How fascinating', growled Tallulah, 'but tell me, doesn't it get in the way when f____?'

As one of her friends once said, 'Tallulah is always skating on thin ice. Everybody wants to be there when it breaks.'

Not reticent about her bizarre habits, Miss Bankhead was widely quoted as saying, 'Cocaine isn't habit forming, darling. I should know. I've been taking it for years and years.'

About the extraordinary opening sequence in Hitchcock's *Lifeboat* when she drifted out of a fog, wrapped in a mink coat, alone in a (what else?) lifeboat, slaving over a typewriter, diamonds aglitter on every wrist, she said, 'They used to photograph Shirley Temple through gauze. They should photograph me through linoleum.'

Bankhead was a fringe member of the famous Algonquin Round Table whose habitues included Alexander Woollcott (the original 'Man Who Came to Dinner'), Dorothy Parker, and anyone else who was literate, witty and influential on the Broadway scene. Who said what to whom has been lost in the mists of time, but a few immortal exchanges emerge regardless of their origin. Tallulah, for example, is credited with nudging the most powerful critic in New York and saying, in the midst of an obscure avant-garde play, 'There is less in this than meets the eye'.

Nor does one know the exact identities of the ladies involved in the following incident at the doors of the aforementioned Algonquin, but when they arrived simultaneously at the revolving door, one stepped back and said with a leer like a lynx, 'Age before Beauty'. The other lady swept straight through and with a winsome smile said over her shoulder, 'And pearls before swine'. Was it Tallulah, Bette Davis, Miss Piggy? Who knows? It will always be a good story.

The Round Table, the epicentre of the New York theatrical earthquake, was a never-ending source of one-line witticisms. When asked what epitaph he would choose for the bed-hopping Miss Bankhead, one of its members suggested that they carve on the lonely tombstone, 'She sleeps alone at last'.

Questioned as to the reason for calling her pet canary 'Onan', Dorothy Parker snapped back, 'Because he spills his seed upon the ground'.

Harpo Marx was spotted one day arriving to join the circle for lunch in a slightly more than dilapidated car. The eagle-eyed Alexander Woollcott saw the rusty heap disgorge its occupant at the elegant entrance and hissed at Marx, 'And what do you call that?'

'This', said a beaming Harpo, 'this is my town car'.

'And what was the town?' asked Woollcott. 'Pompeii?'

The deadly Miss Parker once remarked of a Katharine Hepburn performance: 'She ran the whole gamut of emotions . . . from A to B'.

Indeed Miss Hepburn, though now developed into a monument of the acting profession and one of the world's magical people, seems to have had an abrasive effect on many of her early colleagues. At the beginning of what was to become one of the screen's greatest partnerships, she looked at Spencer Tracy and said, 'I'm afraid I'm a little tall for you, Mr Tracy'.

Spence looked at her for a suitable interval and said, 'Don't worry, I'll soon cut you down to my size'.

Whether it be New York, Hollywood, London, or the Nar Nar Goon Dramatic Society, sheer, unadulterated venom is the blood that keeps the industry alive. In one production I appeared in, the two leading ladies were left alone on the stage for a brief moment. The more glamorous of the pair was called upon to wander round the stage, spot a book resting on the top of a piano, pick it up and say, 'Have you read this, darling? Everyone was reading it on the boat; I believe you just can't put it down.'

I was waiting in the wings and slowly became aware of a long pause and a certain amount of huffing and puffing going on. As a note of desperation crept into the frantic improvisations that were occurring on stage, I considered it prudent to go on and see what misfortune had befallen the deadly duo. I sauntered on to find that the book had been nailed to the piano. No prizes for guessing by whom. The lady in question was sitting peacefully on a divan, puffing at a cigarette, watching her rival tearing at the immovable book . . . and smiling.

Marlon Brando, asked for his opinion of Frank Sinatra, took one of his endless pauses and mumbled, 'He's the kind of guy that, when he dies, he's going to heaven and give God a bad time for making him bald'.

After working with Doris Day in *The Man Who Knew Too Much*, James Stewart, when asked for his reactions, said in his usual laconic way, 'She looked as though butter wouldn't melt in her mouth . . . or anywhere else'. Apropos of the same film, Mr Stewart is reputed to have remarked about his director, the redoubtable Alfred Hitchcock, 'Hitch, on and off the set, is two different people, Mr Hyde and Mr Hyde'.

When questioned about the wisdom of casting an unknown Jane Russell in *The Outlaw*, producer Howard Hughes replied, 'Never mind about her acting ability . . . there are two good reasons why people will go to see her'.

Needless to say, Marilyn Monroe came in for her fair share of comment. After having been dismissed by Laurence Olivier as 'a professional amateur', the poor tortured thing soon read Otto Preminger's comment about her, 'Directing her was like directing Lassie. You had to do fourteen takes to get one that was right.'

The remarks made about the poor girl were enough to drive her to suicide which, indeed, they eventually did. After the sensationally successful *Some Like it Hot*, Tony Curtis was asked what it was like making love to Marilyn Monroe. With a petulant toss of his famous quiff he said, 'It's like kissing Hitler'.

Even those who are supposed to know better have been known to falter. The report on Fred Astaire's first screen test read, 'Can't act. Can't sing. Slightly bald. Can dance a little.'

Bette Davis met much the same fate. On her first visit to Hollywood, she asked why no one had met her and why she had been forced to make her own way to the studios. When enquiries had been made, the lackey who had been assigned to meet her excused himself by shrugging his shoulders and saying, 'But no one who could possibly be an actress got off the train'.

It was a sentiment echoed by the studio, the head of which said, 'I can't imagine a guy giving her a tumble. She's got as much sex-appeal as Rin-Tin-Tin.'

Nevertheless Miss Davis battled on until, after a cascade of Oscars, one of her co-stars was heard to remark, 'No one but a mother could have loved Bette Davis at the height of her career'.

Miss Davis was not alone. Milton Goldman, an agent whose suggestions are taken more seriously than most, had heard rumours of a New York model who might (life is an endless procession of surprises) actually have some talent. Goldman, after seeing the aspiring actress, agreed that there was a tiny talent there struggling to get out and consequently suggested her for the *ingénue* lead in the Broadway production of the enormously successful *Ring Round the Moon*. The director of the play auditioned the actress and phoned Goldman to say that, whilst he thought she was absolutely fine, he was loathe to cast an unknown in the part and had decided to go with an English actress called Stella Andrews. Well, we all know what happened to Stella Andrews, don't we?

But what happened to the girl who was turned down? Her name was Grace Kelly.

Another perceptive talent scout glimpsed Garbo's first test and shot off a cable to her agent which said, 'Tell her Americans don't like fat women'.

On the other hand, agents, in the hope of selling their clients, can weave webs of fantasy that would shame Walter

Mitty. When Harry M. Miller bought the Australian rights to *You're a Good Man, Charlie Brown*, casting director Roland Rocchecciolli was saddled with the unenviable task of finding Australian actors capable of bringing Schultz's beloved cartoon characters to life. The major stumbling block was the casting of Snoopy which, every agent south of Darwin was told, required someone with the manic energy level of Reg Livermore. One Melbourne-based agent called to say that she had just the person but that he was in Brisbane and she would have to find out if he was available. Roland, delighted at this glimmer at the end of his casting tunnel, took great pains to explain that, apart from the essential energy, the applicant must not be more than 34 or 35, which was about Livermore's age at the time.

After days of Roland waiting anxiously, the agent finally called back to say that her client was indeed available. She was hesitant in pointing out that, while his energy level was rather like that of Reg, there might be a problem about the difference in ages.

'Oh', said Roland, 'just how old is your client?'

Replied the agent, 'Eighty-four'.

Hollywood was not averse occasionally to turning the gun on itself. Said Orson Welles, hot from the New York stage and impossible as usual, 'Hollywood's all right: it's the pictures that are bad. They shoot too many films and not enough actors.' Or, on the executive side, 'There's nothing wrong with the place that a dozen first class funerals wouldn't cure'.

As you might have gathered by now, the actor's life is fraught with peril. Not only do his fellow artists conspire to bring him low but the sheer complications of the mechanics that surround him sometimes seem controlled by evil spirits.

I well recall a performance of Olivier's *Macbeth* at Stratford upon Avon when Larry charged up a thirty-foot staircase, and got his foot caught between the solid wood of the stairs and the fragile facade of lathes and canvas that presented a realistic front to the audience. In an instant this skin of illusion began to tear away, firing four-inch nails into the audience like machine-gun bullets while Larry, astride the scenery (very painful), swayed back and forth. Finally, amidst a cacophony of ricochetting nails and ripping canvas, he slid slowly to the stage to be hauled out of the debris by some twenty extras with whom, in fact, he was supposed to be having a duel to the death.

When, in a fit of madness, I allowed myself to be wooed into accepting the part (or parts) of Mr Darling and Captain Hook in London's annual season of *Peter Pan*, I found myself confronted with the problems of wrestling with a vile little boy disguised as a dog; hiding, dressed in a dinner jacket, in a kennel; fighting several sword fights with Peggy Cummins, who barely reached my waist; being blown up by a mischievously planted bomb (I am still deaf in one ear); and walking the plank (still sword-fighting and being eaten by a crocodile). All this brouhaha, however, paled into insignificance when I appeared on the bridge of my ship to find that the ghastly little Lost Boys, plus Wendy, who had been flying round the stage all night like vultures, had finally got their flying wires entangled and were revolving twenty feet above the centre of the stage like some grotesque human chandelier that might have given pause to the imagination of Salvador Dali.

The climax of the first act of that enchanting musical play, *Robert and Elizabeth*, required me to come down a staircase carrying the consumptive Elizabeth Barrett Browning out into the garden for a breath of air, an urge brought on by the first flush of love for poet Robert Browning.

The staging was a triumph, receiving—and warranting—a

standing ovation night after night. As I hefted Elizabeth down the staircase and out through the French windows, enough scenery to mount *Aida* disappeared upwards to be replaced by a horticultural feast of lilac, wisteria and sufficient greenery to keep the Botanical Gardens flourishing for years to come. Simultaneously two delicate gazebos revolved, allowing me, still lugging Elizabeth, to sweep onto the stage with nary a break in the miraculous action. These clever devices were controlled by stage hands crouched on the floor pressing electronic buttons. Having negotiated the staircase with June Bronhill, carried shoulder high and singing like a nightingale, I always looked forward to the moment when I stepped into the gazebo and surrendered myself to the mercies of the assorted mechanics.

On one occasion, however, Miss Bronhill, featuring a crinoline capable of containing a three-ring circus and weighing only slightly less than a Shetland pony, entered the romantic little trellised summer house to find the responsible stage hand dead drunk on the floor in a pool of vomit. Having absolutely no idea of what piece of electronic technology to press or pull, and hearing the leading man, Dennis Quilley, launching into his third version of the show-stopping love-duet, I stamped on everything within reach including the stage hand and the vomit and miraculously connected with something that triggered the whole diabolical device into action. La Bronhill and I whirled onto the stage just as Dennis was running out of words, breath and inspiration. Flinging Bronhill into Quilley's arms, I retreated to the dressing-room for a couple of stiff brandies. Over the sound system, I could hear June and Dennis launch into the love-duet for the nineteenth time. I have never been able to listen to the damn thing again.

Of course films, particularly the films with which I have been associated, are veritable hatcheries of disaster. During the Dance of the Seven Veils sequence in *King of Kings*, Salome, a frightening 15-year-old from Chicago, who fortunately has faded from public view, was required to dance the length of my throne room (a space three times the size of Trafalgar Square) and in a fit of erotic frenzy persuade me to give her the head of John the Baptist, misguidedly played by Robert Ryan. In the course of this marathon, it was decided that she would pull a golden chain that released five hundred budgerigars (yes, budgerigars). These tortured creatures were then to flutter about, filling the throne room and perching on the scantily-clad Salome.

Like all Hollywood fantasies, the sequence took days to rehearse. The flaming torches smoked too much, actors fainted with the heat (a thousand extras on a closed set in Madrid in midsummer), the orchestra couldn't play the barbaric instruments, slaves refused to have their heads shaved and dropped goblets of red wine over $10,000 costumes—in a word, or four, the same old thing.

Eventually we got to the magic moment when Miss Chicago released the budgerigars. As she pulled the chain a great golden globe was supposed to split apart. It did. And not one budgerigar out of five hundred moved a feather.

Some days and many conferences later, it was decided to put a hose into their ridiculous globe-shaped container and, at the moment that Salome pulled the chain, a rocket-like blast of compressed air was to be let loose, literally flushing the poor things out. It worked like a dream. This incredible blast of cold compressed air blowing up their little budgerigar bums shot them straight up to the ceiling where, for all we know, they may still be. Certainly they were never seen again. And neither, I am delighted to say, was the Chicago Salome.

More fortunate, in a macabre sort of way, were the animals that were used in the wolf pit sequence in *The Vikings*. With typical Hollywood wisdom, it was decided not to fill the wolf pit with wolves but, as we were shooting the film in Munich, to use German sheep dogs. As these unfortunate creatures bore absolutely no resemblance to wolves, it was necessary to make them up. This involved shaving them, giving them great shaggy tails, covering them with what in the business is called aluminium dust to make perfectly nice brown dogs look like silver monsters and, finally, fitting them with false teeth (or, more properly, fangs) rather like Lon Chaney Junior in the Wolfman series.

At 5 o'clock on a Munich morning, Kirk Douglas (with a glass eye), Tony Curtis, Ernest Borgnine, Janet Leigh and myself gathered at the pit. There, sure enough, were twenty or so wolves. I told Ernest Borgnine that he was about to be thrown to them and, to give him an idea as to what was in store for him, I stuck a piece of raw meat dripping with blood on the end of a spear and thrust it at the wolves. They didn't move a muscle or snap a false fang. This went on for some time until someone suggested sending for the cattle prods. It did seem possible that a little electric twitch might make these happy creatures, weighed down with more make-up than Mae West, gather themselves together. We were wrong. With false tails wagging and aluminium dust clouding the air, they treated the whole thing as the biggest game since the last Olympics.

It was, by now, deep into the afternoon and we were about to call it a day when some old prop man, who had worked on every film since *Birth of a Nation*, said, 'If you want them to really act up I'll tell you what to do'. I suggested that if he had the magic formula it would have been an act of human kindness to have imparted it at 5 o'clock that morning. This was brushed aside in our eagerness to get some movement out of the beasts.

'If', he said, 'you want to get them to act up, you get a swab of cotton wool, soak it in methylated spirits and dab it on their ass'. Considering the effect that this would have had on Kirk, Tony, Ernest, and possibly even Janet, we agreed. Methylated spirits, cotton wool, etcetera were sent for. False tails were lifted; stinging liquid was applied. The dogs thought it was the greatest fun that they had ever had, which may well have been true. We gave up. We left the wolf pit sequence to the second unit and for all I know the dogs are still sitting in Munich (like the budgerigars in Madrid) waiting for the biggest blast of their lives.

Try as he might to avoid it, there comes a time when, horror heaped on horror, the actor has to face the general public. Not fan clubs; not tame, house-broken, interviewers; but the public, who neither know nor care who he is or what he does. This appalling baptism of fire usually occurs during a tour when he is forced by some sadistic management to hawk his body round the country, selling his latest triumph. During a film promotional tour he is merely required to hover about and be photographable and quotable. During a theatrical tour he actually has to act as well.

Allow Alan Finney, the Rasputin in the Imperial Court of Village-Roadshow, to give you a brief version of the film promotional tour:

'One of the developments accompanying the "renaissance" of the Australian film industry, is the promotion one is asked to do for each celluloid epic. For something called a "renaissance", this involves a particularly old-fashioned form of torture more suited to the times and customs of Attila the Hun.

'I am referring to the publicity tour comprising visits to each capital city of the vast land within the space of five or six days. I'm certain that whoever conceived this gauntlet of gruesome encounters modelled it on the worst horrors of Dante's Inferno where the damned souls reside.

'One is woken in Adelaide at some ridiculous hour of the night—5 a.m.—and immediately carried onto a plane and smiled at by young ladies in uniforms who pour murky hot liquid into one's lap. Some hours later, the aeroplane lands somewhere—one is never told where—and one is pushed off to face 109 pimply-faced boys with pencils, cameras and microphones in their hands, all of whom ask the same question, over and over again. Before one is allowed time to attempt to offer an answer, one is bundled into a car and taken to a large shopping centre—called Indragpilly or some other Aboriginal word meaning 'Let's Get Together and Fill the Trolleys'—and placed on a podium where one is interviewed by a local radio luminary called Waynee Poos whose prime aim in life is to climb the ladder of success using you as his next rung. After being insulted and ignored by this teenager, one is besieged for autographs by a crowd of one or two and, escaping from this milling throng, is whisked away to a local television studio where an earnest interviewer who doubles as newsreader, station manager and cameraman, asks you why you've graced his city with your presence. At this point one is no longer sure.

'From this highpoint, the interview soars into the heavens, reaching an apogee of intellectual achievement with the host of the show informing the world that he really doesn't like Australian movies, isn't going to see this one, thanking you for coming, and finishing with some half-hearted praise of a past performance which only goes to demonstrate that he's confused you with either Leo McKern, Michael Pate or Ron Randell.'

Leading entrepreneur Malcolm Cooke (he was responsible for bringing out Quentin Crisp, who swears that he's going to write a book entitled *Australia . . . And How to Cure It*) shows us yet another side of touring—the 'Pop' tour:

'Before I became a full-fledged producer, I worked for Aztec Services who were heavily into the rock and roll field, and I acted as the tour manager. The headline acts on one particular tour were The Who. They are not only distinguished as one of the great and enduring rock acts, and writers of the rock opera *Tommy*, but were also notorious for their stage act which climaxed with them smashing their guitars and drums into their amplifiers and speakers. We were foolishly under the impression that it was just an act — wrong! By the time they had completed their third concert at the old Sydney stadium, we had twelve smashed speakers and amplifiers which we had supplied. With a full house for the fourth and final sold-out concert the call went out all over Sydney to borrow speakers, amplifiers, spare parts — anything to get the show on. The call was answered and the show started. Our co-promoter on this tour was Harry M. Miller, who appeared for the first time as The Who went on stage. I told him of the horror, mayhem and destruction taking place at each performance and he felt I was exaggerating. I told him to watch. Almost on cue they went into their smashing act. I think Harry must have quickly added up the equipment replacement cost because he went pale and left the stadium, never to appear again on the tour.

'Another Who story occurred when the tour had finished and they were to fly from Adelaide via Melbourne to Sydney and then connect with their international flight to New Zealand. As I said farewell to the Ansett flight bearing them out of Adelaide, I breathed a sigh of relief and adjourned for a pleasant meal and leisurely frolic in my motel with a lady friend of mine. Just as the seduction was about to commence the phone went and I was told The Who had all been off loaded in Melbourne. Subsequent panic phone calls revealed that there had been a beer-can throwing incident on the plane to Melbourne (which, for the sake of the record, was by the Australian supporting act and not The Who) and the pilot refused to carry them. Well the pilot is like the captain of the ship, isn't he? It doesn't matter what the company says, if he won't have you on the plane you don't fly. I kept having this recurring nightmare of The Who remaining in Australia to torture me. After making every sort of plea and threat, including cancelling our Ansett account, I was reduced to begging and finally one pilot agreed to take them to

Sydney under escort of the Commonwealth Police, just in time to catch the last flight to New Zealand.

'Even so simple a chore as touring the enchanting Cilla Black has hidden terrors. One time we were in Perth and we got her out of the theatre straight after the show and drove to her hotel. This was quite close to the theatre and when the fans saw us whip her away they mobbed the hotel entrance. We went around the block a couple of times, fearing they would tear her apart. After the third trip, Cilla said in her charming Liverpool accent, 'I've had enuf of this', opened the limousine door and was out before anyone could move. She just walked straight through the fans with a lovely smile and an 'ullo'. They were so surprised they just parted like the Red Sea.

'One has unfortunate memories of the plane journey that took the Cilla Black company from Hamilton to Wellington, New Zealand. The hotel in Hamilton was one of the quaint olde worlde charming places that did things like serving us all dinner as we got into the dining room at five to seven in the evening, but flatly refusing to serve Cilla dinner as she did not join us until five past seven and dinner went off at seven on the dot. In every room there was a notice to put outside your door each night advising whether you *did* want an early morning wake-up cup of tea at 5 a.m. or you *did not* want an early morning wake-up cup of tea at 5 a.m. I put the *did not want* sign out. Sure enough at 5 a.m. there is a knock on my door, it opens and a cheery face pops in and says, "You don't want a cup of tea!"

'Back to Hamilton airport. We arrived on schedule for our 8 a.m. departure, with everybody grumbling at the early hour. When we got to the airport it was an enormous grass paddock with sheep grazing all over it, a padlocked shed, no person in sight, a funny old 16-seater two-propeller plane sitting with its nose very high in the air and its tail on the ground resting on a small wheel. About 9.15 a.m. someone arrived for the 8 a.m. flight, unlocked the shed and took our tickets. He then opened up the plane and we boarded up a steep 12-foot ladder near the nose. Getting in was like going up the Matterhorn, and getting into our seats was like going down the Matterhorn. The ticket taker got into the cockpit and started the engines. After what seemed like an eternity the tail got off the ground and we were zipping along the grass. White blobs passed by the window, which we realised were sheep. To get into the air the pilot employed the trampoline method. We literally bounced higher and higher until finally we were airborne. There were more prayers offered on the flight than at high mass in the Vatican.'

Here, hot from the perpetually perspiring palms of that peripatetic pixie, John Michael Howson, is the story of a different film star who had a very different fan. As Howson tells it . . .

My television image is one of somebody darting from party to party, champagne glass in hand, picking up tit-bits about the stars which I babble forth whenever a microphone or a T.V. camera is switched on. One thing I have learned when just a pup in business was to avoid asking silly questions or mentioning the obvious . . .

It was Paris. It was Spring. It was a Film Première. The beautiful people of Paris— known for one reason or another as *Le Tout Paris*— were made even more beautiful by Gucci, Pucci and St Laurent, and large bank accounts were there in force. I was in the company of a rather grand expatriate Australian who delighted in naming in as short a breath as possible as many of the titled heads with whom he broke bread.

One of these was a certain Count de X, who gathered a group of people, including the E.A. and myself, into a fleet of cars and spun us to his super elegant home in the super elegant Avenue Foch. The house, a trite smaller than Versailles, featured gilt on gilt, treasures of the family's past glories and evidence that the Count was not exactly on the bread line.

As I looked around the marbled halls and the silken walls, I became aware that they were covered not, as one would have expected, with portraits of the Count's ancestors but with paintings of a gentleman— apparently the same gentleman— dressed as a Grenadier, a highwayman, a cavalier, a pirate, etc., etc. If these are his ancestors, I thought, they were certainly an eclectic lot. The Grenadier, cavalier, etc., all featured a pencilled John Barrymore moustache, more eye make-up than Clara Bow, and a mouth that would have been the envy of Mae Murray, a silent screen star who was known as 'The Girl with the Bee Stung Lips'— or maybe he was just pursing them for the portrait painter.

As the liveried footmen served champagne and delicacies, *Le Tout Paris* wandered around looking like covers of *Vogue International* and *Harper's Bazaar*. The E.A. was absolutely besotted with being surrounded by so many titled people and I was left to make conversation with the Meissen china.

The gentleman featured in the portraits was also featured in scores of photographs which were set in gold and silver frames and placed in rows on every available space. Sometimes moody like Valentino, sometimes hearty like Fairbanks, sometimes staring like Rasputin, his face leered, smiled, grimaced or grinned from every nook and cranny. As I gazed at the photos, my bewilderment must have shown because I suddenly caught the eye of the E.A., who, with panic in his eyes, started to signal me with mouthed warnings, rolling eyeballs and flapping hands. Was he trying to tell me something? I was approached by the Count de X, who had noticed my interest in the photos. Ignoring the E.A.'s strange behaviour I turned to the Count.

'Who is that?' I asked.

There was a pause. The room seemed to vibrate. Glasses crashed to parquetry floors, women swooned and strong men paled. If the French windows had burst open and a

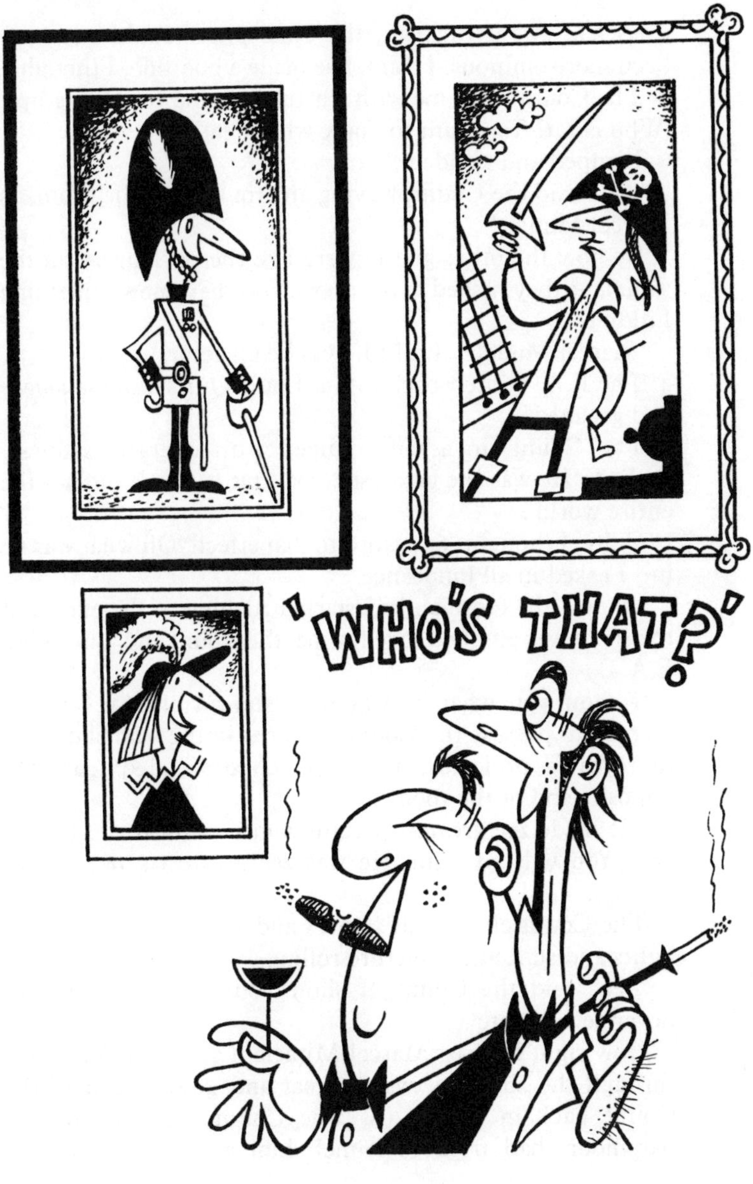
'WHO'S THAT?'

glass had swept through, the atmosphere could not have been more ominous. I think I've made a boo-boo, I thought.

The Count fixed me with tearful eyes and trembling lips. 'Who is zat? You want to know who is zat?'

I gulped and nodded.

'Zat', said the Count, waving an arm around the room, 'is Marcel Miracle'.

By now the other guests were like the passengers on the *Titanic* as they rushed to the doors. Did they know something I didn't?

'Marcel Miracle', I asked, 'was he an actor?'

The E.A. fainted back into a Louis Quinze *chaise longue* and groaned.

The Count, in a voice tinged with operatic sadness, replied, 'He was the greatest actor *dans le monde entier* — the entire world'.

Golly, I thought, or a word to that effect. 'Oh what was he in?' I asked in all innocence.

By now the footmen had started rushing to the exits and the room was emptied save for me, the Count and a moaning E.A.

'I show you what he was in. I show you.' An hysteria seemed to possess the Count. A panel in the wall slid away to reveal a projector, and a screen descended from the opposite end of the room.

'He made zee greatest peectures in zee world . . . I show you. You will love 'im. He was zee greatest star . . . zee *greatest*.'

The Count clicked his fingers and a minion lowered the lights and started the picture rolling.

'Zee', said the Count, 'I show you zomezing you 'ave never zeen before'.

How right he was. Marcel Miracle it seems, as I gleaned through the showing, was a great and good friend of the Count back in the 1920s. The Count, besotted by his paramour, had tried to launch him as a screen star by financing pictures which featured Marcel in every single scene—in pictures which looked as if they had been made on a cold Sunday in the dungeons of the Count's chateau. Not only had Marcel made more pictures than Barrymore, Gilbert, Fairbanks, Valentino, Navarro and other heroes of the silent screen, but he had made more *bad* pictures than anyone in film history.

The flickering epics showed that whatever the above stars could do, so could Marcel—badly! He buckled his swash, trothed his plight and presumably became an instant cure for insomnia, as well as a threat that could have killed the French film industry back in 1924 had the pictures ever been released. The leading ladies looked like Montmartre tarts; the stories, lit by a 40-watt globe, made Goldilocks seem like great literature; and, except for Marcel's gorgeous costumes, the films revealed a paucity of imagination.

In one picture the Count had splurged on a hand-tinting process to provide colour. Marcel looked as if he was suffering from terminal jaundice, the actresses had hard steely eyes, magenta lips and hair that featured all the colours of the rainbow on one head. Driven to drink by the pictures, the hand-tinters had sometimes mis-daubed because eyes ranged from blood red to pea green and sometimes finished up on foreheads or cheeks, while lips seemed to wander from chins to noses with gay abandon.

On and on the pictures reeled. While knocking himself unconscious with a bottle of port, the E.A. occasionally let out a stifled groan which was mistaken by the Count for an ecstatic sigh.

'*Oui, oui*, he is *merveilleux . . . superbe.*'

I sat transfixed, not only by Marcel's performances but by the Count's melodramatics.

'Marcel . . . Marcel . . .', he screamed at the screen. '*Pourquoi partez-vous*? Why did you go away?'

At first I thought Marcel must have dumped the Count for a lucrative offer in a Berlin bordello.

'Marcel . . . Marcel . . . *mon amour* . . . come back, I am waiting . . . I am waiting . . .'

I calculated that Marcel would be somewhere between 65 and death and the poor Count would be better to keep his lost love a fantasy.

'Speak to me, Marcel. *Parle à moi. Je t'attends . . .*'

Nothing issued from the screen through Marcel's pursed lips. Suddenly the Count threw himself on the floor as if before an apparition of the Virgin. Marcel, I presumed, was no virgin but the Count's devotion would have put many a saint to shame.

'Oh Marcel . . . Marcel . . . *mon ange* . . . my angel . . .'

Tears washed the floor. Marcel leered from the screen.

'It was because of zee talking peectures . . . He was ruined . . .'

Remembering that many a Hollywood star had been ruined by a lisp, a stutter, a twang, I waited for the Count to tell me more.

'He couldn't learn the lines. You know, they didn't realize that Marcel acted with his soul . . . not his mouth. How could he speak and act at the same time?' the Count pondered.

How indeed, I puzzled.

'What about writing lines on boards?' I offered, as if Marcel's career could be revived in a flash.

'He couldn't read very well. He never went to school in Bulgaria. When I met him he was just a baggage man—a porter—at the Gare du Nord, but I knew by the way he looked that it was destiny, destiny!' He broke off to sob and pray some more.

'And then he left . . .'

The French Foreign Legion, I thought. Maybe Marcel played Beau Geste for real out on the burning sands.

'He was playing D'Artagnan, on the walls of the chateau, he . . . he . . .' My God he didn't slip and break his neck?

'He met this wealthy American woman and left. *Right in the middle of the picture*! Oh Marcel . . . Marcel . . .'

Presumably Marcel decided on a life where he didn't have to act and speak at the same time.

The sun came creeping in through the shuttered windows and the last film cranked through the projector. The E.A. stirred, the Count lifted himself from the floor and I sat like a stunned mullet. Breakfast was served and we made our dazed farewells.

The E.A. berated me as we tottered down the Avenue Foch. 'Of course I should have warned you. Everybody knows he is obsessed with Marcel. We were lucky; he could have shown us another twenty films.' Obsessed was the understatement of the year.

Some months later I was again swept off to the Count's home, firmly vowing never to mention M.M. I was with the E.A. and a visiting Australian friend, Johnny Kavanagh. We walked into the bubbling party attended by a glittering assortment of free loaders. Suddenly Johnny's eyes swept around the room . . . Too late. He had turned to the Count and before anybody could do anything I heard him ask, eyes wide and innocent, 'Who's that?'

On the theatrical tour, the actor not only has to cope with new theatres, new stages, new hotels and new stage staff, but also with new interviewers, new schools and clubs to be addressed, and new mayors to be patronised by. A one-time mayor of Benalla once slapped Googie Withers on the bottom and said, 'Good on yer Goodge . . . you scrub up better than your photos'.

During one of Phyllis Diller's tours, there was a touch of friction between her secretary, who knew nothing about the Australian scene, and the publicist, who knew everything. Lunching one day in Sydney, the secretary glimpsed someone approaching their table and murmured out of the side of her mouth, 'Oh Christ, here comes another of your geriatric fans'. Ever alert, the publicist rose to her feet, ready to stave off trouble, and then turned to the table with a smile. 'Miss Diller', she said, 'May I introduce Sir Robert Helpmann'. The secretary suddenly found her salad of extraordinary interest.

Googie Withers, who tours more often than a circus, has had the occasional skirmish with the enemy outside, usually in the form of hotels. Incarcerated in air-conditioned planes, theatres, T.V. studios and rehearsal rooms, it is not surprising that she sometimes likes a breath of fresh air. To this purpose she (like many another who shall be nameless) always carries a small screwdriver to open those suffocating aluminium-framed windows that cocoon one in every hotel. Thus equipped, she was touring New Zealand, unscrewing windows and gulping air from town to town. Unfortunately, in one of the more primitive accommodations, the antiquated system could not cope with the added load and exploded. Ever practical, Googie screwed up the hated window again and kept her peace. A year or two later the same procedure was repeated as in an action replay. When, eighteen months after that, the theatre manager rang to book Miss Withers in for yet another stay, the hotel manager said, 'No bloody fear. Every time that woman comes here the air-conditioning breaks down.'

Not fortunate in her choice of hotels, Miss Withers found herself in the lobby of one of our more pretentious provincial pleasure palaces, waiting for her husband, John McCallum, to whisk her away to yet another mayoral reception, when she was repeatedly propositioned by a drunk. Her not inconsiderable patience finally exhausted, she fronted the reception desk and complained. The clerk behind the desk shrugged the matter off. Not one to surrender without a fight, Googie insisted that the minion summon the house manager.

As she waited, she heard the clerk get on the phone and say, 'Hey, Harry, you'd better come down. There's some woman here giving trouble.'

Then, of course, there is the foreign tour, a statistical operation that makes the Normandy Landing look like mumbledy-peg. I proffer a few snippets from my diary concerning a whirlwind whip-around that I undertook for Stratford upon Avon.

I am in Warsaw with the Stratford Company led by Olivier and Leigh, the first English-speaking company allowed into Poland since before World War II. We are a success . . . extra performances have to be given. Olivier and I decide to walk from the hotel to the theatre for a special afternoon performance. In the main street we are brought to a halt by a procession of children going to their first communion, surrounded by priests, choristers, embroidered banners, and sobbing parents. Because it is the first time for years that some semblance of free worship has been allowed, the streets are packed. Larry and I grind to a halt and shed a quick tear as the first two hundred chant past. After five minutes of this, I feel the steely Olivier grip on my wrist.

'Come on', he whispered. 'They might have religion but *we've* got a matinée.'

And I was whisked through the centre of the procession before one machine-gun-armed guard had time to gather himself together.

I walk into my dressing-room in Belgrade to find two men with automatic rifles under their arms, fossicking through my make-up and my costumes. Having already had *eine kleine* contretemps with the border guards and their wolfhounds, I slunk out and questioned the stage manager. Tito and his troupe were attending the performance and, not unnaturally, the secret police wanted to preclude the possibility of the Marshal being shot from the stage. Visions of Vivien pulling a pearl-handled pistol from her garter and emptying it into what was once the Royal Box, flickered across the mind. The performance proceeded with an irate cast—bristling with enough daggers, swords, axes and arrows to overthrow Attila the Hun—shoving the armed guards aside with whispered curses to get onto the stage in time to play their allotted roles. At interval, another crisis: the Marshal and his lady would like to meet the cast but the guards would not let them come back-stage. Would Sir Laurence, Miss Leigh, Mr Quayle and Mr Thring take champagne (domestic) with him in the Box? Up we trek, covered with blood and wounds, to be greeted by an immaculate Tito, hair tinted a ravishing shade of rich mouse with blond highlights, a rather heavy suntan pancake veneer, and a collection of diamond studs, buttons and cufflinks that set off his powder-blue uniform a treat. His eyes combined the best features of both—the diamonds (hard) and the uniform (pale blue). I liked him . . . I know a star when I see one.

I am making *The Vikings* in Munich with Kirk Douglas and Tony Curtis. The studios, about twenty miles from the city, are a model of efficiency. It is Kirk's most expensive independent production—perhaps eight or ten million dollars. A lot of money is being spent, a lot of bonhomie is zinging back and forth. Kirk is glad to get a magnificent studio at a price that wouldn't buy a house in Hollywood; the Germans are glad to have a major film made in their studio, plus the employment of thousands of local extras. Sets are built in a flash, ships are sunk, castles burnt to the ground with a minimum of wasted time. The German executives of the studios glow with delight, dispensing charm and authority with a largesse that borders on the profligate. As I watch

2,000 extras being incinerated in a holocaust of impeccably reconstructed Viking halls, I remark to a nearby assistant that the executives and technicians are running things with great efficiency. He looks at me with amusement and says, 'Why not? They were in charge of Auschwitz.' In the excitement of making my first film in the city where my maternal grandmother was born, I had not realised that Auschwitz was only a morning's drive away.

Vivien Leigh and I are going through our fourth Communist border in two days. Always the guards, the dogs, the watch-towers, the machine-guns, the wire, the questionnaires. Slightly hyped by drinking slivovitz on the Orient Express, we work our way through yet another official form. We do our best, but when we get to 'Religion' those Scarlet O'Hara eyes meet mine and without a moment's hesitation we both shout, 'Druid!' and write it in. It is accepted without question by a thug who would scare hell out of Dracula. And our little joke presumably lies embalmed in some Kafkaesque filing cabinet east of Cracow.

Every actor's nightmare is drying on stage, and not being able to get out of the situation. It does sometimes happen that the stage manager leaves the prompt corner and the actor is left totally alone on stage. Joan Bruce still has nightmares about the time it happened to her.

Joan was appearing in the revue *Airs and Graces* at the Playhouse Theatre in Perth. Throughout the rehearsal she had found the script very difficult to learn. Not only was she single handedly playing four women in a cafe, but the whole thing was written in rhyming couplets.

One night it happened — Joan had a total blackout, and had no idea what came next. For three minutes she sat in the centre of the stage waiting for a prompt which never came. The stage manager had left the corner, and there was no one to help her out. She sat paralysed with fear, unable to move, much less think.

From where he was standing, the stage manager suddenly realised there was a very long and unusual silence happening on the stage. The deathly silence was shattered by the patter of frantic feet running across the backstage area to the prompt corner. Revue scripts are constantly being revised, and they are mostly single sheets of typed dialogue, covered in stage directions and new lines. Joan sat and waited while the stage manager searched frantically to find the right script, which would allow him to give her the prompt. Finally — to the relief of the audience — it came and Joan finished the sketch.

'I would still be sitting there today', she said, 'if he hadn't given me a prompt!'

Shortly before she came to live in Australia, Googie Withers appeared at Stratford with Michael Redgrave in *Hamlet*. One night, just before she was about to go on for the famous 'willow scene', she could not remember her lines.

She turned to her two ladies-in-waiting; one of them was Australian actress Zoe Caldwell and the other was Eileen

Atkins (who created the series *Upstairs Downstairs*). Neither of them knew her first line.

Googie panicked and whispered, 'My line, what's my first line?' They were on a rostrum and far upstage from the stage manager. It was impossible to attract his attention, let alone get a prompt.

Again Googie called into the darkness, 'My line, what's my first line?'

Suddenly out of the darkness and from some forty feet in the air came a thick Warwickshire accent, 'One woe doth tread upon another's heel, so fast they follow—your sister's drowned, Laertes'.

It was a stagehand who had been with the Company for many years and knew almost all the plays by heart!

During her repertory days in the wilds of Wales, Jennifer West—at the age of 22 years—was cast to play the mother in *A Taste of Honey*. The costumes, which were those used in the West End production, were hired for the show. Jennifer West is quite a tall lady—5 feet 9 inches—and she had some difficulty finding anything that fitted! During one performance, as she stood in front of the mirror, she adjusted her hat with a more than usually vigorous bump and grind, and her bottom went right through the back of her very tight outfit.

The audience rose as one man, and Jennifer left the stage sideways!

David Downer and John Stanton appeared together in the Melbourne Theatre Company production of Shaw's *Arms and the Man*, David playing the role of Sergius and John the role of Blunchley. Sergius is considered by many actors to be totally unplayable, and certainly David wasn't helped by his powder-blue and silver uniform which, coupled with his dark, matinee-idol good-looks, made him appear more like the Prince Charming out of a pantomime!

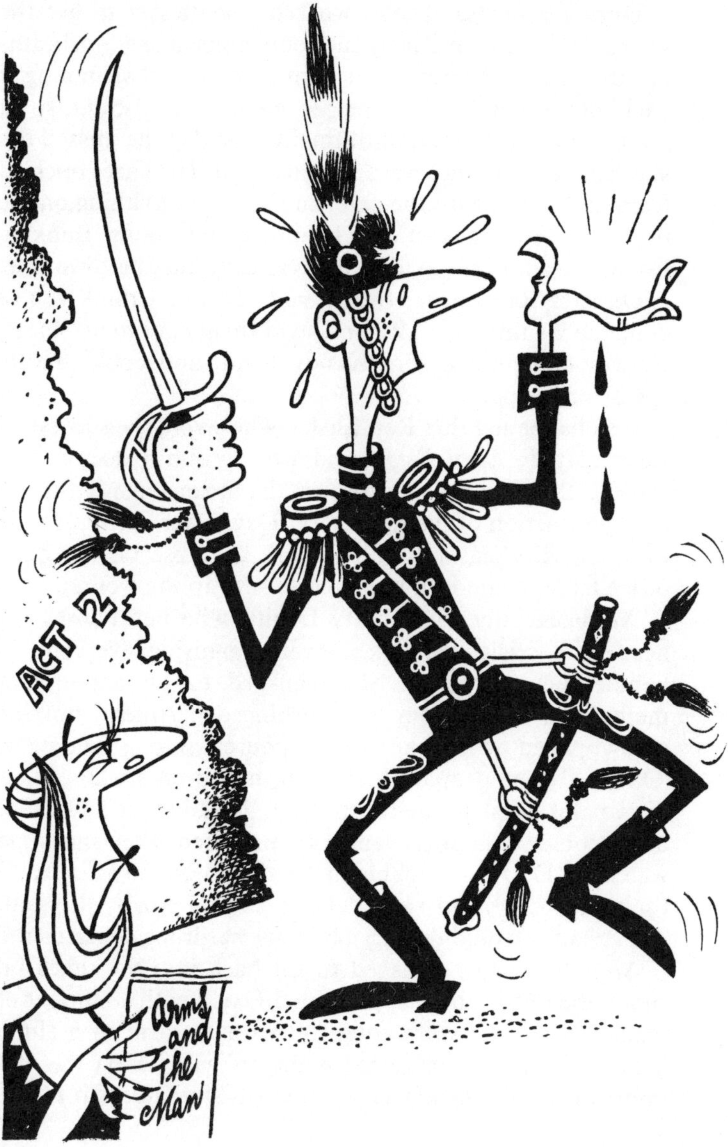
ACT 2
Arms and The Man

During rehearsal David worked relentlessly to get the sword work right, and he spent hours practising at unsheathing the sword, flourishing it with a twirl, and slamming it back into its scabbard. As he became more proficient, so he got more carried away, until finally, one day, he missed the scabbard and ran the sword into his hand. His knees buckled from under him with the pain, and as he lay writhing on the floor, the rest of the cast were hooting with laughter, thinking David was adding even more to his already busy performance.

Director Ray Lawler finally said, 'David, I think you've gone too far this time!' When David finally got to his knees, he was clutching a very bloody hand, and could hardly speak for the pain.

It so happened that Ron Elisha, who wrote the successful stage play *In Duty Bound* and who is also a doctor, was visiting the Company to discuss the arrangements for the first production of his new work. David was carried to the production office and laid out like a corpse on the huge office table, while Ron prepared to sew up the wound.

Wardrobe supervisor Betty Druitt, who never loses her head in a crisis, had taken over organising everyone to handle the emergency. She managed to get a bottle of methylated spirits from the finishing department, but she was appalled when she saw it poured into a container. 'Obviously the people in finishing had been sticking their dirty paint brushes into it', she said. 'It had turned a kind of ochre colour.' She was even more disturbed when she stood watching Dr Elisha cobble at her leading man's finger. 'I thought doctors did such delicate sewing work', she said. 'He certainly wouldn't get a job in my wardrobe department.'

After he finally managed to get back into the rehearsal room, the rest of the cast presented David with a number of medals which he wore complete with his arm in a sling. When he arrived home that night his wife Maria was not impressed, and David's face fell when she said, 'Oh really,

David, just because it's Anzac Day, that's no reason to take the mickey out of all the old diggers!'

David had to unbandage his finger before she would give him any sympathy!

Evelyn Leigh was a big star of the 1940s and 1950s. In her autobiography, *Boo To My Friends*, (Boo being her nickname), she tells of a provincial tour, for which Ken Gregory was the stage manager. In one town, a rather strange man came back to see her after the matinee. Ken, who was a little suspicious of the caller, asked him to wait while he checked with Miss Leigh.

'There is rather a strange man out there asking to see you', he told her. 'Shall I send him away?'

'Certainly not', she replied. 'As long as they want to see me, I don't care how strange they are!'

Ken Gregory is one of the best stage managers in the business. He has worked on masses of shows in Australia, including *Hair*, *Superstar*, the original *Rocky Horror Show*, and *Barry Humphries*, and has also spent some time in England, doing provincial tours up and down the country.

Digs on these tours can be a nightmare, and on a stage manager's salary you can't afford to be all that choosy. When Ken was touring in the Lake District in the north of England, he went to one of the houses on the list provided by Equity. He was shown to a room which was so small it could easily have been used for a cell in *The Nun's Story*. There was a single bed with one foot of space on either side.

Ken took one look and said to the landlady, 'Thank you, but I think it really is a bit small'.

She looked at him for a moment and replied, 'Well, you don't know that when you're asleep!'

Patti Mostyn is one of the funniest women in the business, and she never fails to see the humorous side of every situation—even when the tables are turned on her.

While she was working on *The Michael Parkinson Show*, one of the artists left to her care was film actress Joan Fontaine. On the day of taping, Patti admired a huge pair of diamond and pearl earrings which Miss Fontaine was wearing. Hardly had Patti spoken, than she took them off and presented them to her as a gift. Patti immediately had visions of selling them for millions and retiring. When she got them home, she decided it was time to examine them more closely. Under the light they appeared to be real, so she put them to the ultimate test.

Alas, her worst fears were founded, and Patti ended up with a mouth full of crushed paste pearl!

Joan Fontaine is one of the most amazing women in the business. She always does her own make-up and hair, and she never allows anyone else to do her pressing and ironing because they always rub too hard and reduce the life of the fabric. She is also one of the most astute business women and plays the stock market with great success. Over the years—since she stopped marrying—she has managed to amass a sizeable fortune for herself.

She is also something of an expert when it comes to the English language. Her father was a professor of English, and she has inherited his love of words. As she drove past the Royal Children's Hospital in Melbourne one day she commented, 'That must be a very empty hospital. How many royal children do you have in this town?'

Everyone in the theatre has a recurring nightmare—sleeping through an alarm and missing a performance.

After a Saturday matinee of *The Man who Shot the Albatross*, which starred Leo McKern, the late Lloyd Casey and his fellow stage manager returned to their house in

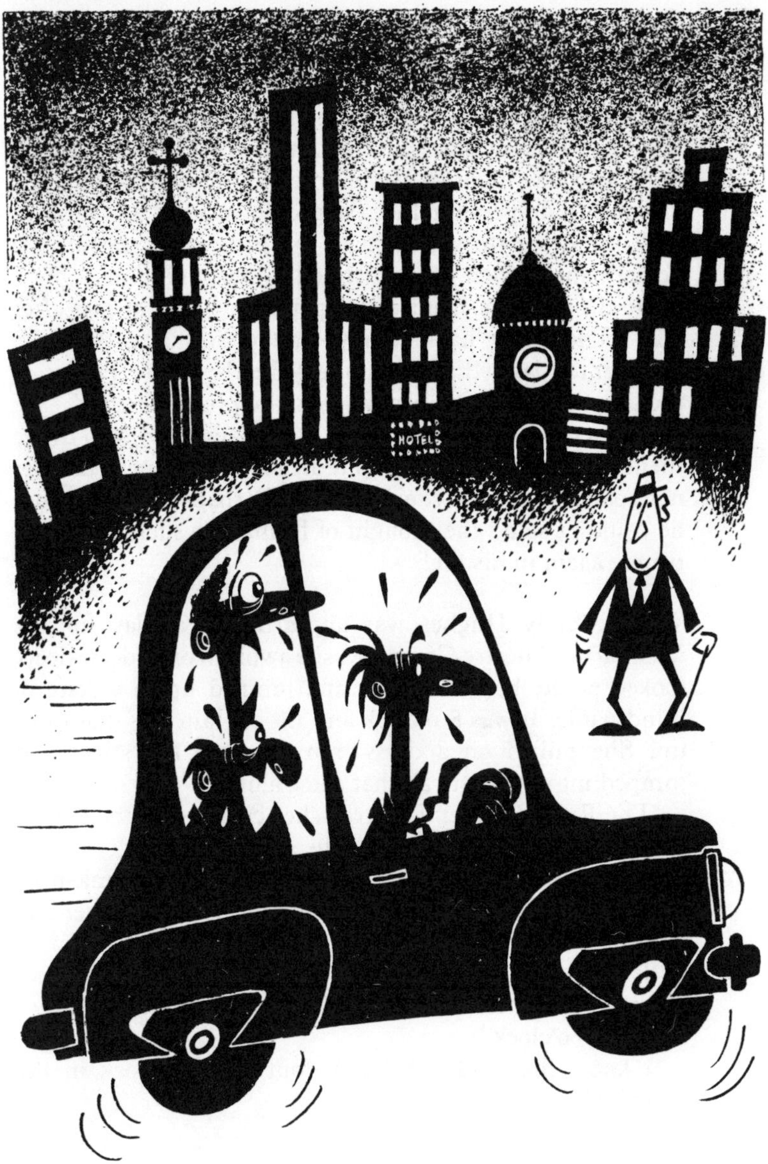
HOTEL

Carlton. It was the middle of winter and, after a meal, they decided to have a kip before the evening show. One of them suddenly woke up at 8 o'clock in a state of blind panic. He called the other, and they grabbed the prompt script and the tapes and ran out into the street, where it was pouring with rain. Saturday night in Melbourne and there was not a taxi in sight. In desperation they flagged down a car, and pleaded with the driver to get them to the Princess Theatre for a performance which was scheduled to start at 8 p.m.

He drove like a maniac and got them there at just after 8.20. The show had already started and Leo McKern commented later that it sounded like the entire Follies as the two ran across the backstage to the prompt corner.

Neither of them thanked the good Samaritan who drove them to the theatre, and despite an advertisement in the *Age* newspaper, he never came forward. Perhaps it was because he couldn't stand the thought of facing two such demented people again in his life!

When Wendy Hughes was appearing in a play for the Melbourne Theatre Company, she awoke from a deep sleep, looked at the bedside clock, and jumped up in a state of blind panic. It was 8 o'clock and the curtain was due to go up! She pulled on a dress, ran out into the street and jumped into the first cab that came along.

'The Russell Street Theatre', she screamed at the driver, 'and make it fast—I'm late for the show!'

The driver eyed her curiously and took off at break-neck speed. When they stopped at the lights he turned to her and said, 'Isn't it a bit early to be going to the theatre?'

By this time Wendy was becoming extremely agitated. 'What do you mean early?' she snapped. 'The theatre always starts at 8 o'clock.'

'I know that, lady', he said, 'but not 8 o'clock in the morning!'

The David Williamson play *Travelling North* proved to be a great success wherever it played around Australia. Jennifer Hagan and Julie Hamilton played sisters, and they went together to David Jones in Sydney to purchase their costumes.

Jennifer went to the maternity department where a very charming, middle-aged shop assistant prepared to take care of her needs. 'How pregnant are you my dear?' she asked Jennifer.

Without explaining that she was appearing in a play, Jennifer replied, 'Nine months'.

The assistant stepped back for a moment, looked at Jennifer with her nineteen inch waist, and said patronisingly, 'Oh no, my dear, I would say two months at the most'.

Quite clearly she thought Jennifer was having a phantom pregnancy.

Monica Maughan was a great success in the stage play, *Three Months Gone* at the Melbourne Theatre Company. As it happens, Monica was three months gone, and did it cause some problems! There were buckets all over the stage and as nature called, Monica would move from one plastic bucket to another. And believe it or not, no one in the audience was aware of what was happening.

Who said you can't fool all the people all the time?

During the early days of the Sydney season of *Boys in the Band* the cast had problems coping with the amount of liquid they were required to consume on stage during the course of the action. John Krummel, who was quite brilliant in the role of Michael, found it most difficult on matinee days when they performed a 5.30 p.m. and an 8.30 p.m. show, with only twenty minutes between shows.

Halfway through the second show — in the middle of Charles Little's big speech — Krummel could contain himself no longer. He moved quietly to the bar, collected an empty Pouilly Fuisse bottle, and went through to what was meant to be the kitchen of the set. Having relieved himself, he left the bottle there, came back onto the stage, and continued with the action.

At the end of the performance, one of the stagehands—who had turned a paler shade of green—came to see John in the dressing-room. He had seen the bottle in the wings and thinking it was grog, had taken a huge swig!

When he appeared nude in the stage play *The Elocution of Benjamin Franklin*, Gordon Chater received a number of letters from the theatre-going public, but one stands out above all the rest.

'I have been a nursing sister for twenty-five years', wrote one woman, 'and in all that time I have never seen anything like it. You have the smallest, ugliest and bluest penis I can remember!'

When the play opened in New York, it followed a production of *The Diary of Anne Frank* into the theatre. At the first matinee Gordon made his famous nude entrance, and one New York, Jewish matron in the front row was heard to say to her friend, 'This is *The Diary of Anne Frank*?'

When Pia Zadora, who has been described as the worst actress in the entire history of the theatre, appeared in *The Diary of Anne Frank*, the critics were aghast. She was so appalling that when the Nazi Germans appeared at the door looking for her, one member of the audience called out, 'She's in the attic!'

I remember saying to Frank Thring during a production of *Batman's Beach Head*, 'Why do you look so different tonight?'

After studying his face for sometime it came to me. He

was wearing his eyebrows for a moustache, and his moustache for eyebrows, and all of them were on upside down!

During *Mother Courage*, which starred the late Gloria Dawn in the title role, and was directed by Joachim Tenschert from the Berliner Ensemble, Frederick Parslow came to grief with a kitchen knife.

Fred was playing the role of the cook, and he got so carried away cutting up his carrots that he sliced his finger. He spent the entire first act dripping blood all over the stage, and in the interval a doctor gave him five stitches, and a big pain-killing injection.

When Frank Thring fainted at the end of the second act of *School For Scandal*, everyone was faced with a real dilemma. Lying there on the stage — looking remarkably like a beached whale — he was far too heavy for anyone to lift. Finally, in desperation, someone had the idea to revolve him off the stage. As he disappeared from sight, the audience cheered. They were also refunded their money! It was the last night of the season.

During the season of *The Time is Not Yet Ripe* (and it never will be for that play!) a telephone bell failed to operate on stage. Actress Elspeth Ballantyne — who has gone on to become a household name in the series *Prisoner* — was on stage alone. Without the call she could not continue the dialogue and a look of blind panic came over her face as she turned frantically for help from the stage manager standing in the wings.

'Pick up the phone', he whispered to her.

In the confusion of the moment — which seemed like hours to Elspeth but was really only a matter of seconds — she stood rooted to the spot. The stage manager had no alternative — and from the wings his voice was heard to call out, 'ring-ring'.

There was not even a titter from the audience as she grabbed for the phone with the human voice.

Autograph hunters can sometimes be a problem, and most international stars have learnt to deal with them. However, there are times when even the most hardened performer is stunned. The late David Niven was confronted in a restaurant by a fan who asked him to sign her petticoat. It was an impossible request to refuse — so he agreed.

Between them they managed to get the task completed, and as she was about to leave she said to him, 'Thank you for being so kind — I have always been a great fan of yours, Mr Rathbone'.

One of the funniest sights ever seen in the theatre occurred when part of the roof blew off the Athenaeum Theatre in Melbourne during a performance. This beautiful old theatre was taken over by the Melbourne Theatre Company, put back into good working order, and used as their classical main house. During the period it had been dark, pigeons had moved in and roosted in the fly tower above the stage. The gust of wind that unsettled the roofing also disturbed years and years of pigeon droppings.

However, the actors did not miss a beat in the dialogue of *School For Scandal*, as they wandered around the stage in their periwigs and beauty spots, covered from head to toe in pigeon droppings.

Boys in The Band was one of the most controversial stage plays ever produced in this country — and it was also one of the most successful. It was the first play to deal with the theme of homosexuality in explicit terms. The play opened in Sydney at the Playbox Theatre and toured all over Australia. It was in Melbourne that the now infamous trial took place, and several of the actors, including John

Krummel, convicted of using indecent language in a public place.

In Brisbane, a woman came backstage after a performance and asked to see the stage director. Before he could open his mouth, she turned on him and said, 'I just want to say that I saw the Vienna Boys Choir, and they were much better than you'.

Before the stage director could answer she had turned on her heel and left. It took him some time to work out what she meant. Clearly she thought The Boys in the Band were a singing group, and sadly they had not come up to her expectations!

Betty Druitt, the wardrobe mistress at the Melbourne Theatre Company, has been known to strike fear into the heart of the most difficult actors. She has been heard to shout at an actor, 'Come late once more to a fitting, and you will go on stage naked'. Stage managers have been known to tremble in fear when she raises her voice.

An actress who had been warned by Betty about her particularly delicate costume, failed to heed the words of warning. On the opening night, after several dress rehearsals, she appeared trembling before Betty with an enormous tear in her silk skirt. Betty eyed the disaster for a moment then said to the actress, 'They tell me you are a very good actress — I suggest you use your talents and mime a mend!'

On another occasion, the publicity man at the Melbourne Theatre Company was standing idly chatting to Betty, who was quite obviously up to her eyes in costumes for a Restoration comedy.

'Please go away', she said in a tone which everyone has come to recognise. He ignored the warning signs and went on chatting. The tension mounted, and Betty repeated her plea, 'Please, if you don't go away, I shall throw the cutting shears at you'. He hesitated for a moment too long — and throw the shears she did! They missed their target and went into the curtain behind him, leaving a five-foot tear as they slid down to the floor.

The story is still told at the Melbourne Theatre Company—and Betty maintains she never meant to make contact.

The stories about actress Jennifer Clare are never ending. She has a reputation for being vague, as well as a very talented performer. She has been known to fall out of French windows from the first floor of a mews and land in the cobbled lane below. She walked away with only severe bruising.

Betty Druitt remembers being called into the Russell Street Theatre one evening to find the dressing room in total chaos. Jennifer was playing the lead in *Cat Amongst The Pigeons*—one of those parts where she was required to look a million dollars.

'It was like something out of *Cinderella*', Betty recalled. 'The stage manager was trying to squeeze Jennifer's feet into a pair of shoes which appeared to be three sizes too small.'

In fact, Jennifer had such bad tinea that her feet had swollen and the shoes no longer fitted. Betty looked for a moment, saw the humour of the situation, and said, 'What you need, Jennifer, is a pair of wellies filled with Dettol!'

Not all the stories of the theatre are funny; some are just plain remarkable. Sir Robert Helpmann—the first knight of the Australian theatre—is one of the least starry actors, and he is also very funny. There is nothing he will not do to promote a show, and he never complains about a work load.

Sir Robert has had the most wonderful career, and there are few people in the business with whom he has not worked. He is reluctant to talk about himself, and even more tight lipped about those he has worked with. He has no plans to write an autobiography. 'I have never told the truth about myself', he says. 'Why should I tell it about other people?'

One story he did tell, however, is well worth repeating. During the Second World War, Sir Robert, like many other stars, joined the Army as part of ENSA (Every Night Something Atrocious, as it became known) and was sent to Europe to entertain the troops.

'It was fantastic', he recalls. 'We performed on the back of trucks and did two performances a day of *Swan Lake*.'

Sir Robert and Dame Margot Fonteyn were performing in the lowlands of Holland in the region where the Waal and the Rhine rivers meet, when word came through that the Germans were advancing. The Dutch plan was to burst the banks of the dikes and flood the area to slow down the troop movements. Both Sir Robert and Dame Margot were terrified but continued the performance without interruption. At the end of the show a very elegant woman came onto the stage and made a long and patriotic speech. When she had concluded, a small girl presented Sir Robert and Dame Margot with bouquets. By the time they left to make their way back to The Hague where they were billeted, the water was already rising up around the wheels of the bus.

Many years later, Sir Robert was in Hollywood and a very beautiful and talented actress asked him if he remembered the incident. 'Indeed I do', he replied.

The child had grown up to become Audrey Hepburn. The woman who had made the long speech was her mother, a baroness, who was also the leader of the Dutch Resistance Movement.

One day in Melbourne, Sir Robert noticed a Council utility drive by. The back of the vehicle was filled with potted flowers which were being delivered to various public gardens, and the sight triggered a memory for him. 'That's how they got us out of Holland. They covered the top of our vehicle with potted tulips so that the aircraft would not notice us from the air.'

For years now the Rudas Dance Company has been touring *Snow White and The Seven Dwarfs* around Australia and New Zealand. While the artistic standard of the show has sometimes left a little to be desired, there is no denying it has been a great success, and presumably a big money winner for Rudas.

On a trip to New Zealand, one of the Dwarfs contracted an illness which precluded him from appearing in the show for some considerable time. Rudas was faced with a dilemma. He had no understudy for the performer, and he was certainly not in a position to cancel the show. In a moment of brilliance the answer came to him.

He changed the name of the show to *Snow White and The Six Dwarfs*.

Musical comedy star Nancye Hayes was leaving the stage door of Her Majesty's Theatre in Melbourne when she was greeted by two adoring fans.

'Oh Miss Hayes', they enthused, 'that was such a loverley fillum!'

'Thank you', the ever-gracious Miss Hayes replied, 'but it wasn't a film. We were up there performing live for you.'

Obviously star struck at the sight of the lady, the two took absolutely no notice of what she was saying to them. 'Oh yes', they went on, 'but we didn't know it was going to be in colour. All the pictures outside the theatre are black and white.'

Kenn Brodziak is one of the most successful entrepreneurs in Australia, and he is also known as the man who brought the Beatles to Australia. He has presented a long list of shows and artists over the years, and he has an international

RUDAS DANCE CO.
present
SNOW WHITE AND THE SEVEN DWARFS
SIX
CINEMA

reputation as one of the smartest producers in showbusiness. His stage shows include *Pippin*, *Charley Girl*, *Godspell*, and *Canterbury Tales*.

Kenn was awarded the Order of the British Empire—OBE—for his services to the performing arts. It is often joked in the business that OBE stands for old, bald entrepreneur! Here are a few stories from Kenn.

Marlene Dietrich, who toured Australia in 1965 and 1968, ranks as the most stimulating and exciting personality I have dealt with. One night at The Princess Theatre, Melbourne, when we were talking about food and exchanging recipes, Marlene said, 'Have you ever had kidneys cooked in French champagne?' I replied, 'No, but it sounds wonderful'.

'Well if you like', she offered, 'I will come and cook them for you at your home on the first Sunday I have off'.

About a week later on a Friday, she rang me and said, 'Don't forget I am coming to cook kidneys in champagne for you next Sunday, so will you order the kidneys and make sure they are veal kidneys. You can ask whoever you like and I will do all the cooking and serving, but I will not sit down and dine with you.'

Sunday duly arrived and at 11.30 a.m. there was a ring at my front door and when I opened it there was Marlene. She had a package in each hand. 'What's that?' I asked. She replied, 'That is a carving knife because I know you bachelors never have sharp knives'.

'What's in the other hand?'

'That is the French champagne—I brought my own because I have stirred all the bubbles out of it and that is the only way to use it.'

Marlene then proceeded to the kitchen and cooked luncheon for six. She was the complete *hausfrau* and she duly served us a most delicious meal, after which she collected and washed up all the dishes. My guests and I were amazed at seeing the glamorous Marlene in such a role.

I had tried for more than three years to engage Sidney James to come to Australia and do a show for me but had been unsuccessful. In 1974 I was in London and I again asked Sid's manager about his availability. He told me Sid was performing in *The Mating Season* in Eastbourne, and suggested we drive down and ask him if he would like to go to Australia. We drove to Eastbourne and I saw Sid in the show and afterwards we dined at the leading hotel there. Sid was very jovial and delightful company but he was quite adamant that he did not want to come to Australia. I was equally determined to entice him here and at the end of the meal I had a brain wave. I noticed Sid had only eaten seafood, so whilst we were having coffee I asked Sid if he liked oysters.

'I adore them', he replied.

'Sydney has the most succulent oysters in the world', I said. 'Do you like crayfish?'

'It's one of my favourite foods', says Sid.

I replied, 'Victoria and Tasmania cannot be beaten for them. And how about prawns? Australia leads the world in prawns.'

'Prepare the contract, I am coming to Australia', Sid said.

And that is how I got him for his first tour, after which he returned for two subsequent tours and every time he ate little else but Australian seafood!

I brought Liv Ullman, the famous Norwegian star, to Australia in 1977 and on the Saturday night before her opening asked her if she would like me to give her a little dinner party, to which she replied in her charming Scandinavian accent, 'What I would like most of all is to come and cook for you and the director and cast'. I told her that would be fine, so Liv cooked her speciality, spaghetti and clam sauce, at my penthouse, for eight people. It was absolutely delicious.

I reciprocated by cooking Steak Diane for the same eight

people the following Saturday after her show. Incidentally, my Steak Diane is a great favourite with Derek Nimmo, who has come to Australia so often. The recipe for this dish was given to me, when I was a young man, by its creator—a waiter at Romanos, a leading Sydney restaurant which faded from the scene many years ago.

Although it is over twenty years since I signed up The Beatles, I am still known far and wide as 'the man who brought The Beatles to Australia'. Whilst we were in Brisbane, the famous four told me they would really love to try some typical Australian food—something you can't get anywhere else. I went to great pains to get them some witchetty grubs and Moreton Bay bugs. The boys refused to sample the witchetty grubs, but they did relish the Moreton Bay bugs, despite their name!

Carol Channing has an allergy which requires her to drink only special water and eat organic food. When she arrived in Australia in 1972 she was accompanied by dozens of enormous bottles of water, plus special foods, and trying to get everything through Customs and then to her apartment needed a small army of helpers.

Prior to her visit, I had endeavoured to find a source of organic food for her and my search took me to Gippsland where I found a farmer who produced organic lamb. He was most co-operative when I told him I needed some for Carol Channing and he told me he would deliver it to me. However, I got the surprise of my life when trucks kept arriving at my home with whole organic lambs, plus organic vegetables which he had grown. It was almost a full-time job for a cook to get freezers in which to store all the food and then to cook it for Carol.

On Carol's first Sunday here, she told me she would like to see a movie. I arranged to meet her at a city cinema at 8 p.m. to see *Clockwork Orange*. A few minutes before eight

I was waiting for Carol when someone came up and started talking to me. I said, 'I'm sorry I can't talk to you now as I am waiting for Carol Channing'.

The person replied, 'I *am* Carol Channing!'

It was impossible to recognise Carol in a trench coat and a man's hat, as without her wig, eyelashes and make-up she didn't look anything like the Carol Channing I had previously known and seen on stage and in films.

I brought Sophie Tucker to Australia in 1962 to appear at the Tivoli Theatre and we became firm friends. A ritual developed with Sophie which was called 'Tucker at Midnight'. This took the form of a small supper party two or three nights a week at the then famous Menzies Hotel, when Sophie would act as hostess to about a dozen friends and V.I.P.s in her suite after the show.

I well remember Sophie's first words to me when I met her on the tarmac at Essendon as she alighted from the plane. She was surrounded by press photographers and TV cameras and she quickly whispered in my ear, 'Don't let the TV get any close-ups—it will hurt your box office'. The wise Sophie knew she was no chicken and that television cameras can be quite merciless for people of her age.

Many people ask me about my most successful shows and it is hard to pick from such hits as *Godspell*, *The Black and White Minstrel Show*, *Charlie Girl*, *A Chorus Line* and *Annie*, but I can tell you that my smallest success was *The Jack Benny Show*, which I presented in the early 1960s. This did sellout business in Sydney but failed to attract large audiences in Melbourne with the end result being a profit of 10 shillings!

The best entrance and exit lines came from Bette Davis, who was in Australia in 1975. Her first line on entering the magnificent concert hall at the Sydney Opera House was, 'Boy, what a dump!'

When I said goodbye to her in her dressing room after her last show at the Dallas Brooks Hall in Melbourne, she asked me if I would call her when I was next in New York so that we could have dinner together. I said, 'Fine, what's your telephone number?'

She replied, 'My number is 226 9071'. A long pause and then, 'And the name is Davis'.

One of my favourite stories concerns Winifred Atwell and her many concert tours here in the early 1960s. Winnie was known as 'The Queen of the Keyboard'. She was not in the least temperamental but she could be difficult sometimes about pianos. One night the stage manager came and asked me to go and see Winnie as she had said she would not perform because the piano wasn't good enough and she was breaking her nails hitting the keyboard.

I went around to her dressing room and she said, 'I won't go on'.

'Yes you will', I said.

She retorted, 'No I won't'.

I insisted, 'Oh yes you will'.

'And why will I?' she demanded.

I replied, 'Because there are £3,000 pounds in this packed house and you are getting half and that is why you are going on'.

She then unsheathed her dazzling smile and replied, 'You are quite right you know'.

Stories of George Bernard Shaw are endless and everybody has one.

Of the institution of marriage he said, 'It is so popular because it combines the maximum of temptation with the maximum of opportunity'.

His longtime friend and actress, Mrs Patrick Campbell, said of marriage, 'It is the longing for the deep, deep peace of a double bed, after the hurly-burly of the *chaise longue*'.

Margaret Trudeau said of her then husband, Canadian Prime Minister, Pierre Trudeau, 'He has the body of a 25-year-old'. Spike Milligan, who was on the same television programme with her, added, 'Yes, and he keeps it in the refrigerator'.

Spike Milligan said of the army, 'It works like this: If a man dies when you hang him, you keep hanging him until he gets used to it'.

Groucho Marx complained, 'I once chased a woman for almost two years, only to discover her tastes were just like mine — we both adored girls!'

Woody Allen observed, 'Sex between a man and a woman can be a wonderful thing — providing you get between the right man and woman'.

Rod Stewart complained, 'How dare they describe this thing I have worked at in my voice box as "shouting". I always feel my voice is like black velvet on sandpaper.'

A journalist who had trouble getting Cary Grant to take his telephone calls, sent him a telegram asking for clarification of his age.
  'How old Cary Grant?' the telegram read.
  'Old Cary Grant fine. How you?' came the reply.

Dorothy Parker said, 'I was the toast of two continents — Greenland and Australia'.
  When told at a Halloween party that people were ducking for apples, she commented, 'There, but for a typographical error, is the story of my life!'
  'Give a man a free hand, and he'll run it all over you', she once told a gathering of ladies.
  A woman once took Dorothy Parker to task and accused

her of being terribly outspoken. 'Outspoken by whom?' Miss Parker questioned.

American critic Walter Kerr wrote of the play, *I am a Camera*, on which the musical *Cabaret* was based, 'Me no Leika!'

Robert Garland wrote of Chekhov's masterpiece, 'If you were to ask me what *Uncle Vanya* is about, I would say — About as much as I can take!'

Bette Davis commented of an available young starlet in Hollywood, 'She was the original good time that was had by all'.

'Equity Blacks Othello' screamed the newspaper headlines, when British Actors' Equity withdrew Paul Robeson's membership.

When Gertrude Lawrence appeared in the stage play *Skylark*, George S. Kaufmann reviewed the production and described the event as, 'A bad play — saved by a bad performance'.

Haywood Braun wrote of a new play on Broadway, 'The play opened at 8.40 sharp, and closed at 10.40 dull'.

Sir Robert Helpmann commented on *Oh Calcutta*, 'The trouble with nude dancing is not everything stops when the music does'.

Georges Simeon — the creator of the *Maigret* series, was asked if it was true he had made love to 10,000 women.
　'Yes', he replied, 'I went back and counted'.

Wrote one critic of a production of *King Lear*, 'The actor playing the king spent the evening looking as if he were under constant fear that someone else was about to play the ace'.

Guido Natzo was in a nondescript Broadway production, and one critic wrote, 'Mr Natzo was not so Guido!'

Sammy Davis Jnr, when asked about his golf handicap, replied, 'I'm a one-eyed black American'.

Sir John Gielgud was having difficulty being heard over the orchestra of an opera he was directing. Finally, in desperation, he was heard to shout, 'Do, do stop that too dreadful music!'

Sarah Bernhardt — the great tragedienne — was tearing the set apart and destroying furniture as she turned in her performance of *Cleopatra Queen of The Nile*.

'How different, how very different, from the home life of our own dear Queen', one of the English matrons in the audience was heard to comment.

Musical comedy star Nancye Hayes took her neighbour's children to see a production of the ballet *Swan Lake* at the Sydney Opera House. The two children, Jacinta and Alexander, sat through the four acts with hardly a movement.

At the end of the performance, the two soloists were presented with a sheath for the ballerina and a bottle of champagne for her partner. Later at home the children were asked what they thought. Jacinta was full of the tu-tus and the swans, while Alexander remained silent. Finally he said, 'It was all right. At the end, the bloke jumped off a big rock into the lake, and got a bottle of scotch for doing it.'

For almost her entire career in the musical theatre, Nancye Hayes has been confused with veteran musical star, Evie Hayes. During *Sweet Charity*, the show in which Nancye was such a success, she received a letter from a fan who was so looking forward to seeing her in the role.

After all—her mother remembered her from when she was a little girl!

Raymond Massey, during the time he was playing Abraham Lincoln on Broadway, became somewhat involved with the part. A friend was heard to comment, 'He won't be satisfied until someone assassinates him!'

Bebe Daniels and Ben Lyon were big theatre stars in the 1930s through to the 1950s. On one occasion, they were flying from London to New York and after several hours in the air, Miss Daniels began asking how long before they arrived at their destination.

Eventually she explained she was desperate to spend a penny, but she refused to use the aircraft lavatory. 'I can't possibly go in there', she explained, 'there are no curtains on the windows'.

When Googie Withers made her entrance in *Woman in A Dressing Gown*—wearing no make-up, her hair in rollers, and scratching her behind—a woman in the front row was stunned. 'My God', she exclaimed, 'hasn't she gone off!'

Jennifer Hagan and John Stanton were starring in the Melbourne Theatre Company production of *Electra*, which was directed by Frank Hauser. The costume designs were by Anne Fraser, and she dressed John in what he described as 'a pleated skirt' and which he hated. However, the costume did show off to advantage John's very good legs. One matinee he strode onto the stage to confront Jennifer as Electra, as she stood surrounded by her seven ladies-in-waiting.

A woman in the front row was heard to say, 'Oh, it's John Stanton'.

'Really', her friend replied, 'which one?'

John hated the costume even more after that!

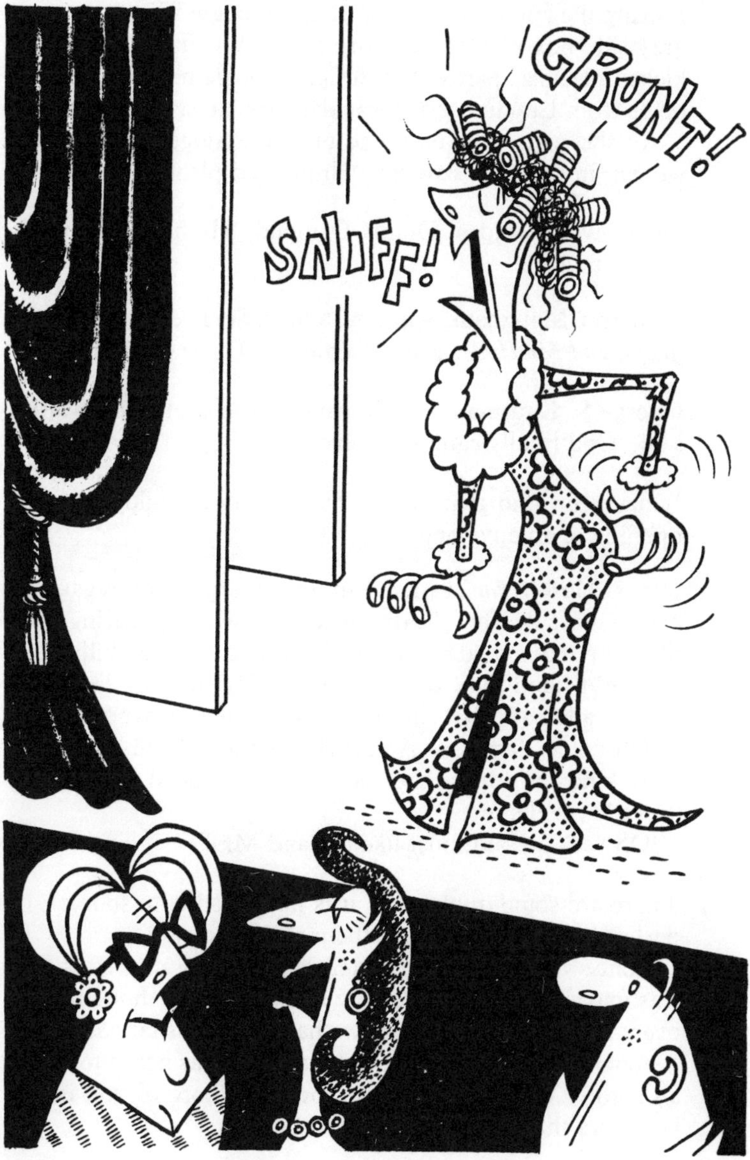
GRUNT!
SNIFF!

During the run of *Simon and Laura*, Googie Withers wore a grey silk, box-pleated shirt dress, which featured hemmed-kicked pleats as part of the design. Googie had brought the dress from London and it was the very latest in fashion.

As she made her entrance onto the stage, she heard a woman in the front row say, 'Unpressed pleats!'

Orson Welles said of Donny Osmond, 'He has Van Gogh's ear for music'.

Somerset Maugham, while watching Spencer Tracy in *Dr Jekyll and Mr Hyde*, asked, 'Which part is he playing now?'

George S. Kaufmann, on hearing of the death of a waiter, said, 'God finally caught his eye'.

It has been said that actress Sylvia Miles would go to the opening of an envelope.

James Mason was caught up in an argument regarding billing outside the theatre where he was appearing. Mr Mason remained adamant that he would not take billing on the right-hand side of the awning. His leading lady was equally adamant that she should have the left-hand billing.

'Oh come, James, it is normal for the lady to go first in these kinds of things', the management pleaded, attempting to settle the dispute.

'Oh yes', he said, 'just like Mr and Mrs!'

There are some quotes that it is not possible to source — or perhaps it is safest to leave them anonymous!

I once heard an actor in Melbourne say to an actress who was making certain requests, which clearly he thought were over the top, 'I didn't know we had divas this far south!'

Again in Melbourne, a stage manager was heard to say to an actor, 'My dear, there are fourteen more of you in the lane, and they are all waiting for a job!'

A star actress was looking through the costume designs for a classic period play in which she had agreed to appear. Looking at one hat design, she said, 'I can't wear that — it looks like a cook's day off!' The designer went absolutely ashen with anger — and the actress never did wear the hat!

A Perth actress arrived at the first day of rehearsal and was asked by the stage manager if she had her lines down: 'Yes', she replied caustically, 'both of them!'

A Sydney director was giving a stage manager a hard time during the technical rehearsal. Unable to stand the abuse any longer, he threw his headset down onto the stage and said, 'I'm sick of you. When you have need of a stage manager, call me! I'll be in the bar.' With that he went off and left the cast and director to get on with the last act without him.

A Melbourne stage manager dismissed an actor before the director had finished rehearsing a particular scene.
 'Go out and find him', the director called.
 The stage manager left the building, waited some minutes and came back.
 'It is 5 o'clock on a Friday afternoon', he said coolly, 'and there are three million people out there and they all have a story.'
 With that he sat in the prompt corner and refused to move.

A fireman at the Comedy Theatre in Melbourne stood watching the stage manager working and then commented, 'You're a funny lot, you thea-raticals!'
 On another occasion, an actor had to jump between the same stage manager and a drunken fireman when he started to unbuckle his axe to attack him.

During the Melbourne Theatre Company rehearsals of *The Man Who Shot The Albatross*, which starred Leo McKern and was written by Ray Lawler, director John Sumner gave the stage manager three or four replacement soldiers to rehearse at the Princess Theatre.

One of the actors—who shall remain nameless—went to him before the rehearsal started and asked if he could douse himself with methylated spirits. Rather perplexed, the stage manager said he had no objections, but wondered why.

'Since I am playing one of the soldiers who was involved in the Rum Rebellion, I think it would help me find my character if I could smell the alcohol on myself', he explained.

This same actor had an equally ridiculous problem in the middle of filming *The Cherry Orchard* at the ABC in Melbourne. Just as he was about to shoot his big scene with Googie Withers and Wendy Hughes, he rushed up to the stage manager with a maniacal look in his eye and said he had lost his character.

Both his parts were non-speaking.

The Melbourne Theatre Company production of *Sons of Cain* starred Sandy Gore, Liddy Clark, Max Cullen, John Gregg and Noel Ferrier, while David Williamson wrote and directed the play.

Noel Ferrier was asked by an interviewer whether his character—a media mogul—was based on Lord Beaverbrook, Rupert Murdoch or maybe one of the Fairfax family.

'Certainly not', said Noel, 'I decided that as the media baron was tough, heartless, cruel and ruthless it would have to be done properly. So I modelled it on Ita Buttrose!'

Jennifer West played the principal boy in Edgar Metcalfe's production of *Dick Whittington*—and stunning she was too! She fought *Young Talent Time*'s Johnny Young for the hand of the Princess—and won!

The big love duet for Jennifer West and Rosemary Barr—who was playing principal girl—was 'If I Gave You' from the *Fantastiks*. During the rehearsal Jennifer could not get all the gifts in sequence, but by opening day she almost had them sorted out. One day, however, Rosemary Barr nearly died laughing when Jennifer sang of giving her, 'Rings of diamonds, silver buckles for her shoes—and a school of flying octopii . . .'

Jennifer sang on without missing a beat!

The Playhouse National Theatre in Perth toured a production of *Altona* around Australia, starring Peter Collingwood, Eileen Colocott, Rosemary Barr, James Beattie and Edgar Metcalfe, who also directed.

James Beattie played the part of the rather dotty German son who was locked in the cellar and fed on champagne and oysters. Empty oyster shells, together with copies of German newspapers, which had been obtained with great difficulty from the German Embassy, were left scattered all over the floor of the cellar. The oyster shells were very important as the character spent part of the night talking to them.

In Brisbane the theatre cleaners were so meticulous one night that they swept up the oyster shells and the newspapers and disposed of them. Stage manager Ken Gregory arrived at the theatre to find not only that the oyster shells and newspapers had gone, but that the theatre rats had eaten through the birthday cake—leaving only the candles behind.

With only thirty minutes before curtain time, Ken made some frantic telephone calls to a seafood restaurant in Brisbane and the problem of the oyster shells was solved. Copies of the *Courier Mail* doubled as German newspapers, but the cake was not replaced.

The Hole in the Wall Theatre in Perth is a stunning little in-the-round theatre. Edgar Metcalfe recently directed a production of *Dracula* for them, starring Ivan King.

Since the theatre has no house curtain, and the audience totally surround the acting area, all the scene changes are done in low level lighting, in full view of the audience. To transform the study into the cellar, the furniture was covered with dust covers. The stage management also placed a coffin in the centre of the playing area, and then Ivan climbed in.

Edgar—who was playing the role of the little man who eats the flies—was hiding underneath one of the covers, waiting to leap out at an unsuspecting victim. One night he suddenly found Ivan attempting to hide with him under the dust cover.

'What are you doing?' he whispered to Ivan.

'I can't find the coffin', Ivan replied in a state of total panic.

'Well, get out—you can't stay here', Edgar said laughing uncontrollably, as he pushed him away.

Ivan stumbled around in the darkness, and when the lights finally came up he was in place in the coffin.

Edward My Son is a play by Robert Morley which deals with the problems of alcoholism. When it was first performed in London it starred Robert Morley and Dame Peggy Ashcroft.

Edgar Metcalfe co-starred in an Australian production with Peter Collingwood. Peter had a habit on stage—which anyone who has worked with him will know—that could sometimes send scenes a little awry. Edgar played the role of Edward and Peter the role of Harry. In the final scene, Edward, holding a teddy bear in one hand and a drink in the other, offers Harry a drink.

'Harry, have a drink', he says. Edgar, however, was having such trouble controlling his laughter, he offered him the teddy bear. Unable to control it any longer, the two actors stood facing each other and laughed openly! The audience enjoyed it as much as the actors.

Ron Graham, Joan Bruce and Peter Collingwood were appearing in *A Member of The Wedding* at the Playhouse in Perth. Peter Collingwood was sitting in his dressing-room waiting for his next entrance. Suddenly he heard a long silence, and jumped up from his chair and rushed to the stage. Ron Graham, who was in the middle of his big scene with Joan Bruce, became aware of the sound of frantic feet on the stone steps leading up to the stage.

Behind him on the stage he heard the door open and a voice say, 'Oh Christ!' and the door closed again. Peter had made his entrance several pages too early!

Peter Collingwood is one of the finest actors in this country. He has a wicked sense of humour and the most marvellous sense of the ridiculous. He also happens to be a very fine director, and a true man of the theatre.

During the run of the *Cat and The Canary* — which is really rather a dull thriller — he took to playing the most marvellous pranks. At the end of the act, his body would be discovered in a cupboard, and as the door was opened he would fall out — face first — onto the stage.

Each night the death was different. One night his hair was standing straight up as though he had died from fright; the next night he would have a rope around his neck and a huge orange tongue hanging from his mouth. Another night he had ping-pong balls hanging down onto his cheeks, looking as though his eyes had popped right out of his head. His face was always suitably contoured and grotesquely made-up. Fortunately the cast were all facing upstage when this took place, and the act curtain prevented the audience from seeing their laughter.

Every stage manager's nightmare is a mechanical device that fails to work during a performance. During a production of *Macbeth*, which Edgar Metcalfe directed in Perth, the designer came up with the ingenious idea of having a bat that flew from one side of the stage to the other. Well—one night it happened! The bat—which ran on a wire rather like those money-carrying devices one used to see in department stores many years ago—got halfway across the stage and stopped.

Despite much pulling and tugging by the mechanist it refused to move—and there it stayed for the entire performance, looking remarkably like Lady Macbeth's medieval black knickers hanging out to dry!

Frank Baden Powell directed a production of *Cat On A Hot Tin Roof* at the Playhouse in Perth, with Ron Graham playing Brick and Eileen Colocott playing Maggie.

One night they wheeled on the birthday cake, complete with the required number of lighted candles, and proceeded to sing Happy Birthday to Big Daddy. By the time they got to the end of the song, the top of the cake—which was made of cardboard—was completely ablaze.

Showing great presence of mind, Eileen picked it up, carried it off stage, and flushed it down the loo on the side of the stage.

The sitting-room of the set for *Cat On A Hot Tin Roof* was dressed with a chandelier, which was flown out during the day while rehearsals for the next play were taking place on the stage.

The actor who was playing Big Daddy turned to Ron Graham (Brick) and said, 'You see that chandelier there?'

Ron Graham, realising they had forgotten to fly it back in, paused for a moment and said:

'No'.

There was a moment of uncertainty, and Big Daddy, who managed to control his laughter replied, 'Well, it was there yesterday'.

Cat On A Hot Tin Roof proved to be a nightmare for stage manager, Ken Gregory.

'There's a mighty big storm brewin' up, Mr Pillott', the man servant said.

Mr Pillott, dressed in his pyjamas and dressing gown, moved out onto the balcony to watch the storm clouds gathering on the horizon. Somehow he managed to get the cord of his pyjamas tangled up in the iron lace-work, and he could not free himself. He played the whole scene shouting his lines back into the sitting-room, while he was manacled to the balcony!

Edgar Metcalfe was artistic director at the National Theatre at the Playhouse in Perth, and he was the man who gave me my first job in the theatre. An Englishman, who served his apprenticeship in repertory theatre in England, he was a strict disciplinarian, and a very talented director. I learnt more from him than anyone else in the business.

Edgar cast me as a soldier in *Henry IV* parts I and II. I shall never forget the look on his face when I arrived on the morning of the first dress rehearsal with platinum blonde hair.

'It wasn't much better when it turned carrot red', he said years later, 'and it certainly didn't make you look any shorter!'

Fortunately he didn't have time to rehearse another soldier or I would have been out of a job. It was the motliest collection of soldiers you ever saw, headed by strapping John Orcsik, who had recently won the title of Mr Perth. After looking at my skinny legs hanging out of the bottom of a tabard, with John next to me looking like Hercules, I pleaded to Edgar, 'Do I have to stand next to him?'

At school matinees the audiences of kids saw the humour and would cheer when we made our appearances. We never failed to get scores of wolf whistles and pelted with Jaffas. I have never heard more laughter for a Shakespearian play.

Edgar was playing the king as well as directing. On opening night, he slipped on the stage, which was very heavily raked, and ended with his legs in the air facing the audience.

The audience found it very funny, especially as they could see that the mail he was wearing—knitted string painted with silver frost—ended just above his knee. While Edgar was standing, the tabard he was wearing prevented this from being seen by the audience.

Spread-eagled on the stage, with the silver mail ending just above his knee, the great expanse of human flesh, and the black knickers exposed to all, he looked like something out of a strip club.

It was in this production of *Henry IV* that the late Alf Hurstfield had to take over the role of Falstaff from Neville Teede only weeks before the opening. Alf was rather a short man and he looked very funny with his ruddy face and a huge 'belly' padding which seemed out of proportion to the rest of his body.

In the recruiting scene, Alf had to approach the six-foot tall John Orcsik, place his hands on his shoulders, push him to his knees and dangle his broadsword over his cod piece saying, 'I'll tickle your catastrophe'.

The only catastrophe was that Alf couldn't reach John's shoulders, and he ended up looking like a bull mastiff trying to mount a great dane from the wrong end!

Mr Brown Comes Down The Hill was a very effective piece of theatre, superbly directed by Edgar Metcalfe. One night, the black American actor who was playing Mr Brown (alias God), failed to show up at the theatre. With only five minutes' notice, Edgar had to black up and go on. Since he directed the production, he almost knew the part, and was able to carry the script under his arm without the audience knowing.

The actor eventually turned up at interval, with the

excuse that he had slept through the alarm. Edgar, who was far from amused, said, 'Well you can just go around and watch it from the front — I am not taking all this off now!'

Peter Wyngarde came to Australia to star in the stage play *Butley* — and it was a resounding flop! Unfortunately it had been a long time since Peter had been on stage, and his success as Jason King in *Department S* failed to draw the crowds.

John Frost was stage manager, and one night he took up the Act II curtain without checking to see if Peter and Arna Maria Winchester were ready for the action. Peter was caught centre stage with his finger up his nose! He stood rooted to the spot for a moment staring at the audience, and then gathered himself together and got on with the play. He was furious when he came off at the end of the show and called John 'a bloody amateur!'

Knowing that he would be reported to the management, John was in the Harry M. Miller offices at 9 a.m. the next morning relating the whole story to Garry Van Egmond, who thought it was hysterical.

Hugh Colman is one of the most talented set and costume designers in Australia. He designed the Melbourne Theatre Company production of *An Ideal Husband* starring Googie Withers — and a stunning design it was too. The set was made from what appeared to be pale blue marble, and never failed to get a round of applause when the curtain went up.

The play was set in England in 1880, and the opening costume Hugh designed for Googie was quite extraordinary, featuring heavily draped and garlanded hips. After the first full dress-rehearsal, Hugh was asked to go to Miss Withers' dressing-room at the Comedy Theatre.

Since it was Hugh's first big production, everyone, including John McCallum, was trying to be very tactful.

'Do you think you could do something about the sides of the gown? It is very lovely—but perhaps it is a little much.' What he was really trying to say was Googie looked like a galleon in full sail.

There was a silence for a moment and then Googie turned to Hugh and said, 'My dear, I look like Widow Twankey!'

Hugh also designed a production of *Sleeping Beauty* for the Australian Ballet, which was playing at the Sydney Entertainment Centre. The role of the Prince was being danced by an Australian who had only recently returned from England, and he was feeling very nervous about his debut.

Invariably when the artists don't get something right they blame someone else, mostly the costume. After missing several of his *grande jettes*, the dancer stopped and called out into the auditorium, 'I can't breathe in these tights!'

'Fine', Hugh replied, 'I shall get you some tights you can breathe in'.

The first production I ever worked on at the Melbourne Theatre Company was *The Life of Galileo*, directed by John Sumner and starring Frank Thring as Galileo. The rehearsal was a very exciting time, and I think it is one of the shows which I have enjoyed most over the years. There were some quite magical moments created by John Sumner, which, coupled with the set by Kristian Fredrikson, and some very clever lighting effects, held the audience spellbound.

Frank had a huge role, and very early in the rehearsal period he started to work without the script. One morning he seemed to pause—for a very long time—so I gave him a prompt, thinking he needed some help. Nothing! I gave him a second prompt; still nothing. The third time, thinking he had not heard me, I gave him the line—this time very much louder. He lifted his head from his hands, stared at me for a moment and said, 'I know—I'm acting!'

Ian Cookesley, who is now the Production and Technical Director at the Melbourne Theatre Company, was the production stage manager for *Hair*. He and the other stage managers who worked on a number of productions for Harry M. Miller were sometimes also landed with the technical details of other promotions.

Back in 1969, mineral water was just becoming a fad in Australia, and Harry M. became involved with Hepburn Spa — and it almost drove everyone mad. Harry M. decided he was going to have the biggest launch Sydney had ever known for Hepburn Spa. He wanted a glass swimming pool in a restaurant filled with mineral water, and a girl swimming naked throughout the luncheon.

Ian finally found a place called The Grotto, which had to be seen to be believed. He felt like one of the children at Fatima, and kept waiting for the apparition to appear. Unfortunately he couldn't get enough mineral water to fill the pool, so it was just plain water. However, Hepburn Spa is carbonated, so Ian had to arrange for the bubbles in the water. Instead of oxygenating the water, he used carbon dioxide which reduced the temperature of the water very quickly.

The poor girl was nearly frozen to death as she swam around, smiling for the press.

It was also Ian Cookesley who painted the seats of the Jane Street Theatre with leather lacquer instead of vinyl lacquer. The lacquer failed to dry, and when the ladies stood up at interval they left their dress patterns on the seat.

'Well, at least you could tell who was wearing cheap fabric!' Ian said years later.

Back in the late 1960s, Jon Ewing was sitting in a very fashionable coffee lounge in Macleay Street, Kings Cross, watching the world pass by. Seated at the table next to him were a group of Carnaby Street trendies, who had come to the Cross for their Saturday night entertainment.

Jon suddenly became aware of an obviously drunk passer-by standing with his nose pressed up against the plate-glass window, attempting to focus his bloodshot eyes. Jon turned to see what he was staring at and noticed that one of the females in the group next to him was wearing her blonde hair piled so high on her head that it seemed to defy all the laws of gravity.

After some moments of disbelief, and several attempts to focus his eyes, the drunk moved on.

Suddenly — as if from nowhere — the drunk was standing at the table next to Jon. He stood swaying for a moment and when he finally managed to focus his eyes on the blonde, he said with a slur, ''Scuse me, lady, but I think your head's exploded!'

Otto Preminger is one of the nicest people in Hollywood and New York — very funny and amusing, and not at all like the ogre he is sometimes made out to be. He has been responsible for a number of successful careers, and he has also ended several others.

When he made *The Man With The Golden Arm*, he cast Frank Sinatra and Kim Novak as the leads. Way back in those days he paid $100,000 for Miss Novak, but what they neglected to tell him was that all her films had been dubbed because she couldn't speak the dialogue. Such an idea was against all Preminger's principles and training. He was determined Novak would say the words, and so he ignored all her pleading, crying and hysterics.

'Frank was marvellous', he said. 'Sometimes we did as many as thirty-five or forty takes, but in the end she did it.'

It was he who drove Tom Tryon from the screen after they made *The Cardinal* together. 'He wasn't a very good actor, but he is now a very successful writer', Preminger remarked.

Preminger saw Clifton Webb on stage and wanted him for his film *Laura*. He knew he was right for the part, but Darryl

F. Zanuck made all sorts of unpleasant remarks about Webb being effeminate and wouldn't hear of having him in the film.

Preminger eventually wore Zanuck down. Webb not only got the part, he became Zanuck's closest friend, and the biggest star at 20th Century Fox.

When Preminger came to cast *St Joan* he saw 18,000 hopefuls, and eventually settled on Jean Seberg, whom he found in the mid-west of America. She turned out to be one of his less successful 'punts'. Some ten years later he was accosted by a stage mother who was still furious that her daughter had not got the role. 'You didn't recognise talent when you saw it', shouted Barbra Streisand's mother.

Preminger is the man who discovered Linda Darnell in *Forever Amber*; fired Lana Turner when she refused to wear a pair of 'off-the-peg' slacks; gave Lee Remick the break that turned her into a star; packed John Wayne off to war in *Harm's Way*; turned Paul Newman into an Israeli in *Exodus*; took Frank Sinatra to the depths of despair in *The Man With The Golden Arm*; and gave George C. Scott his first movie role. He also dared to engage Dalton Trumbo to write the film script of *Exodus*, even though he had served a jail sentence for 'anti-American activities'.

He is the man who refused to remove the word 'virgin' from his film *The Moon is Blue*. He took the Hays Office to the Supreme Court—and won.

One critic wrote of him, 'If there was any justice in the world today, Otto Preminger would be a bar of soap'.

Following years of speculation, Otto Preminger, after the death of Gypsy Rose Lee, publicly admitted that he was the father of her son and has since legally adopted him.

John Orcsik appeared in a production of *Johnny Belinda* at the Patch Theatre in Perth, in which he played the role of McCormack, who is shot dead at the end of Act I. John had been cast in the role—sight unseen—because, as the director put it, 'He was the only one big enough to play the dumb part'.

As the season progressed, John's death became more and more extended. From first being shot on the second step, he eventually managed to get himself onto the landing before Belinda fired both barrels into his back. Having just won the title of Mr Perth, his young ego started to get in the way of his ability, and he believed he was invincible — capable of leaping over tall buildings in a single bound, and bouncing down staircases without spilling a drop of human blood. During one performance, after taking what seemed like an eternity to die, he flung himself backwards with such dramatic gusto that he pulled the entire staircase away from the wall and landed centre stage in a tangle of splintered steps and busted balustrade.

'I don't care what you do to yourself, but please, don't destroy the set!' the director said when he came backstage during the interval.

Guns on stage are a constant nightmare as they always seem to misfire at the wrong time. They can also be extremely dangerous when put into the hands of careless stage management and inexperienced propsmen.

At the same time the gun shot rang out in *Johnny Belinda*, John Orcsik was aware of something whizzing past his ear at a great pace. While lying dead in the centre of the stage, he opened one eye just enough to be able to study the set at the top of the staircase. There — in full view for the audience to see — were two quite large holes where the wadding from the blank cartridge had embedded itself in the flat. The propsman had forgotten to remove the wadding from the cartridge before he loaded the shotgun!

Perth actress Margaret Ford was appearing in a production of *Romeo and Juliet* at the New Fortune Theatre in the grounds of the University of Western Australia.

The New Fortune, a replica of Shakespeare's Globe, is an open-air theatre. At the dress rehearsal things went well for Margaret as she sat embroidering a huge screen.

What they failed to tell her for the opening night was that the stage manager had sized it (tightened the fabric with a thin, all-over glue solution), which made it impossible to push the needle through. Facing a full first night audience, Margaret battled as she determined to get the needle through and complete the embroidery. The audience were fascinated by her endeavours as the action continued around her.

Suddenly, ringing out like a bell in the still summer night air, the voice of Neville Teede was heard to say, 'Margaret makes all her own clothes!'

Actress Nita Pannell was appearing in a production at the Playhouse in Perth. Suddenly during rehearsal she stopped and looked to the director for help.

'Do you think it would be possible for my partner to speak a little faster?' she asked.

'Why?' the director enquired.

'Well, you see, I am folding this newspaper during that speech, and he is still speaking when I have finished folding!'

The cancellation of an opening night is something which has rarely happened in Australia, but it occurred one night at the Community Theatre in Sydney (now the Marion Street Theatre). The play, a comedy called *Out of The Crocodile*, had in its cast Ron Falk and Joan Bruce playing the husband and wife, Kirsty Child and Peter Adams playing the romantic leads, and Anne Haddy playing a 16-year-old — complete with gym tunic, long plaits and painted on freckles.

At about 6 p.m., Sydney was hit by torrential rain, and the entire metropolitan area seemed to be covered by six inches of rushing water. Transport stopped, cars were washed away, and electricity supplies were cut off everywhere. For several hours the entire city ground to a halt as the rains continued to bucket down.

With little or no relief in sight, the actors set out for the theatre which is located in Killara on Sydney's North Shore, about ten miles from the centre of the city. Ron Falk found himself stranded on Milson's Point railway station. Peter Adams was stuck in a train in Wynyard tunnel, and in desperation he jumped off and ran back along the tracks to the station. A stupid action in hindsight as he could have been killed by a train coming in the opposite direction.

Anne Haddy was stranded on Pacific Highway with a broken down car. She positioned herself on the median strip in the centre of the Highway and attempted to hail any car that would give her a lift to the theatre. Kirsty Child somehow managed to arrive at the theatre about 7.30, looking like a drowned rat. Joan Bruce, who lived just a short distance away, had a broken down car; and Alex Archdale, the director of the theatre, set out to pick her up and ended up getting his car bogged. Eventually Joan's babysitter drove them both back to the theatre.

By about 9.15 p.m. the entire cast had finally arrived at the theatre. Of the invited 400 guests, only 70 managed to make it. Alex went out onto the stage and made a short speech. He gave the audience a choice of either starting the performance at the late hour, or going into the foyer to have a drink and coming back the next night. The decision was unanimous— they had a drink and came back the next night.

The season turned out to be a great success—when eventually the play opened.

The Community Theatre production of *Richard III*, starring Peter Adams and Rod Mullinar, was indescribably bad, and most of the cast hated doing it. There is an Equity ruling which states that if there are more members of cast than audience, the show can be cancelled. Every night the cast counted, hoping they would be able to cancel.

At last it happened—there were fifteen in the cast and only twelve in the audience! The actors could not get out of their costumes and make-up quickly enough. The thought of a night in front of the television was more than they could believe!

During the run of the musical *Robert and Elizabeth*, June Bronhill always wore a black opal and diamond ring. One evening, after having been to a function during the day, June forgot to change to the normal ring. For some reason Frank Thring—who was playing her father—noticed the difference, and it caused him to smile. June saw his reaction and decided that from time to time she would get him.

From then on she wore all sorts of rings, including huge pearls which she purchased from Coles, tied onto her finger with bits of string, and bandaids covered in glitter. In the end Frank wasn't brave enough to look at her hand, and June would do everything within her power to make sure he saw it!

June Bronhill has the most wonderful sense of humour, and she constantly tells stories against herself. Her recollection of her first audition at Sadlers Wells—which she tells complete with various characterisations—could easily be a revue sketch. One of her first appearances at Sadlers Wells was in the role of Gilda in Verdi's *Rigoletto*.

The death of Gilda at the end of the opera leaves Rigoletto, her father, absolutely devastated. June decided she would employ that rather clever theatrical trick to die with her eyes open. As he sits cradling his dead daughter in his arms, Rigoletto twice calls out her name, as though willing her to live.

'Gilda, Gilda', he wailed, at the same time spitting straight into her eye. As she lay there motionless with an eye full of spittle, June vowed she would never again die with her eyes open!

June Bronhill, Jon English and Simon Gallaher co-starred together in the re-vamped version of Gilbert and Sullivan's operetta *The Pirates of Penzance*, which became known simply as *Pirates*.

Having learned that Major Stanley is not an orphan as he declared, the Pirate King (Jon English) is determined to see justice done. 'Our revenge shall be swift, and terrible, and...'

'Sweet', replied Ruth (June Bronhill), as it had been scripted.

As the season of *Pirates* progressed, Jon began adding more and more adjectives to describe his revenge.

Enjoying the joke, June decided to get him one day. After he had gone on at great length describing his revenge, she waited and then added—sounding like Robert Newton playing Long John Silver, complete with Worcestershire burr and contorted face—'Di-abol-ical!'

Jon did the slowest take in the world, looked at her long and hard, and said, 'What did you say?'

June repeated it, 'Di-abol-ical!'

The audience, who were in on the joke, cheered and stamped. On the closing night, determined to get Jon for one last time, June waited while he went through the whole long description and then added, 'Dish-pic-able', sounding exactly like Sylvester the cat. Jon was unable to contain himself for laughter.

One of the most successful plays presented at the Hole in the Wall Theatre in Perth, was a piece called *Turn on the Heat*. It was based loosely on the last three hours of the life of Marilyn Monroe, and it was a one-woman show in which Eileen Colocott was absolutely sensational. The character in the play was called Marilyn Marlowe.

The piece was a monologue, and the action took place in her bedroom, with all the dialogue centering around a series of telephone calls. The telephone was connected up to the prompt corner, and it allowed the stage manager to talk to Eileen if she got into trouble with the words, or if she lost her place.

Interestingly, the part was so absorbing for Eileen, that she never knew when she had taken a prompt. She would come off at the end of the show and ask if she had taken a prompt. In most instances she could not recall it happening.

Jennifer West and Arthur Dignam were in a production of *Twelfth Night* at the Octagon Theatre, in the grounds of the University of Western Australia. Jennifer, who stands 5 feet 9 inches tall, with a mane of Titian hair, made a stunning looking Viola, while in the disguise she made a not bad looking fella!

In the famous ring scene when Malvolio, in a fit of pique, throws the evidence to the ground and accuses Viola most vilely, she replies with the equally famous speech,

'I left no ring with her: what means this lady?

Fortune forbid my outside have not charm'd her!'

Michael Rolfe, who was playing Malvolio, threw the ring so hard it bounced off the stage, and ended up under the feet of the audience in the front row. Jennifer was left with no alternative but to retrieve it. Without the ring the scene could not proceed, and there was no one else on stage to get her out of the situation.

For several minutes Jennifer ad libbed, 'What ring my Lord? I see no ring', while, down on her hands and knees, she crawled around lifting up the feet of the audience, trying desperately to locate the missing link in the story. To make her plight even worse, Jennifer is as blind as a bat and cannot see inches in front of her face without her glasses.

When eventually a gentleman in the front row located the ring and handed it back, Jennifer was laughing hysterically. 'Thank you my Lord'—and on she went to deliver one of Shakespeare's famous soliloquies.

Simon Chilvers was appearing with the Melbourne Theatre Company in a production of *Blythe Spirit*, which was directed by Bunney Brooke. Simon, who stands 6 feet tall and is built like an athlete, was playing the role of the husband. He had one particular speech which started with the line: 'When I was a little boy . . .'

One night— lost in the wilds of Victoria— for no apparent reason, he suddenly said, 'When I was a little girl . . .'

Harry M. Miller's production of *Present Laughter*, with Stuart Wagstaff, Rosemary Martin, Sue Becker, and Patricia Leahey, was one of the last shows to play at the beautiful old Palace Theatre in Sydney.

After its Sydney season, it went out on a national tour, which used to be normal practice. Half way through act one at the Hunter Theatre in Newcastle, there was a total power failure. For a few minutes the audience sat in the pitch black, and then out of the velvet darkness came the voice of Stuart, calling for the usherettes to turn on their torches and come down to the edge of the stage. He had the stage manager bring in the house curtain and for the next twenty-five minutes— with the torches shining in his face— Stuart regaled the audience with his old front cloth comedy act. 'They adored it', he said. 'In fact, the play was an anti-climax after the comedy turn!'

The next time Stuart appeared at the Hunter Theatre was in *There's A Girl in My Soup*. This time the power supply did not fail, but during the day a violent storm blew away one wall of the stage area. A tarpaulin was strung up, and the actors, who could hardly hear themselves for the beating rain and the constant 'flap-flap' of the tarpaulin, soldiered on.

Christine Amor, who played the role of Felicity in the Crawford series *Carson's Law*, was married in a most beautiful restaurant garden in the Dandenong Mountains, just outside

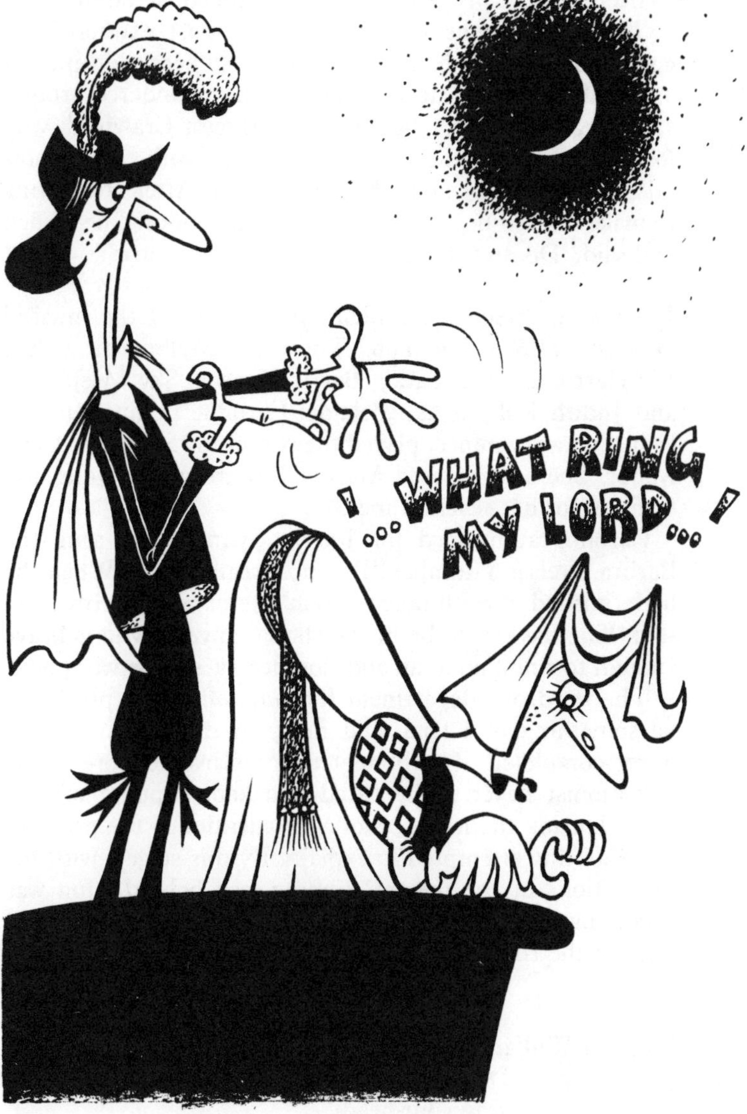
'...WHAT RING
MY LORD...'

of Melbourne. It was a very small affair, with only a handful of friends and Christine and Mark's immediate family.

The photographs were taken by a most extraordinary couple. The female half of this double-act kept shouting out and making a great deal of noise as they wandered around snapping away with a box brownie. Hector Crawford, who lost part of his vocal apparatus in a battle with cancer, now talks in a most appealing hoarse whisper. After attempting to make himself heard over her constant shouting, he turned and said, 'Doesn't she know they're silent pictures!'

Jon Ewing directed a brilliant production of the musical *Guys and Dolls* at the Total Theatre in Melbourne. It had Liz Harris as Sister Sarah, Barrie Hope as Sky Masterson, and Judith Roberts as Adelaide. Caroline Gillmer, in her first stage appearance, played the role of the Salvation Army Major. She also covered Marion Edward as Big Jule, and went on for her several times.

Caroline auditioned for Jon in Sydney, and sang the Barbra Streisand number, 'I'm the Greatest Star'. When she had finished the number, which she sang superbly, Jon said, 'She has got to be in the show — anyone who is brave enough to sing that at an audition deserves to be working'.

The wardrobe department for *Guys and Dolls* proved to be something of a trial, and many of the costumes were never completed. The bonnet which Caroline wore as the Salvationist never really fitted and kept slipping off her head. During the note session, Jon mentioned the problem and Caroline attempted to explain. By this stage — with the renovations of the theatre running way behind — Jon was becoming very short tempered. 'I don't care if you have to Ramset the thing onto your head', he snapped at her, 'just fix it'.

Director William Wyler, who is Bette Davis' favourite, once yelled at her, 'Do you want me to put a chain around your neck? Stop moving your head!'

Errol Flynn and Bette Davis were never great friends. While he was the stud of Warner Bros. Studios, he starred or co-starred with everyone — with two exceptions, Bette Davis being one.

On one occasion he said to the great lady, 'I would love to proposition you, Bette, but I'm afraid you would laugh at me'.

Never one to miss the rare opportunity to agree with a man, she replied, 'You're so right, Errol'.

The filming of *Dark Victory* was a very trying time for Bette Davis. The pressure of her recent divorce caused her, after a week of filming, to approach producer Hal Wallis and offer to give up the role. She explained that she was extremely upset and felt she was unable to do justice to such a wonderful role. Mr Wallis — who had seen a week of her work on the screen — replied, 'Stay upset'.

She eventually won an Oscar nomination for her performance. However, the Oscar went to Vivian Leigh for *Gone With The Wind*.

Shelley Winters was preparing to see Darryl F. Zanuck about a big role in an important film. Zanuck's reputation for womanising was well known, and he never missed an opportunity for a conquest. 'Miss Winters', the reporter said, 'we hear Mr Zanuck chases beautiful young girls around his office, and tears off their dresses'.

'Really?' she replied. 'Okay, so I will wear an old dress.'

It has been alleged that while making the film *From Here to Eternity*, Ava Gardiner said, 'We are making a film about the end of the world, and what better place to make it than here in Melbourne.'

Ava did not say that at all. It was a made up quote from a reporter who had failed to get a comment from the actress when she arrived for the commencement of filming!

However, it is true that Ava refused to curtsey to the

Queen when she was presented at a Royal Command Performance.

Over the years Googie Withers and John McCallum have done much to foster Australian talent. It was John McCallum who fought—and won—against the Williamson's board and cast Jill Perryman in the lead role of the stage musical *Funny Girl*. Later he cast Nancye Hayes in the role of *Sweet Charity*.

John and Googie also helped an international artist on her way to stardom. They were at a nightclub in Paris, and as they watched the dancing troupe who were part of the floor show they noticed the tall, dark haired girl on the end of the line. They both agreed she had something which set her apart from the other girls.

The next morning John telephoned his agent and suggested he should look at her. The agent took John's advice, went to the club, and eventually signed the tall, doe-eyed dancing girl.

She turned out to be Audrey Hepburn!

The stage musical of *Gone With The Wind* never really managed to get off the ground. When the production opened in London, Sir Noel Coward was in the audience.

The dread of every actor is appearing on stage with animals and children—and given a choice of either, they would be hard pressed to make a decision. *Gone With The Wind* had both! A blonde, ringletted, toe-tapping child and a Clydesdale which pulled the buggy during the burning of Atlanta scene. The child was especially obnoxious, and the horse got stage fright and dropped a huge pile in the centre of the stage.

Sir Noel turned to his companion and said, 'If they took that child and shoved it up the horse's backside, they would kill two birds with one stone!'

Actors and designers are constantly at each others' throats about the way they are going to look. 'If that's what I'm going to wear, I shall have to re-think the whole part', actors have been heard to say on countless occasions.

Bette Davis has never been one to sit back when she felt something was wrong for her performance. The film *Marked Woman* called for Miss Davis to be beaten almost to a pulp, and her face scarred for life. The director handed her over to the make-up men for bandaging, and when they had finished their task she felt she had never looked more attractive. The creamy puff of gauze was a millinery masterpiece, and was something she could have worn to Ciro's nightclub. However, it was certainly not convincing as a bandage.

During her lunchbreak she went to visit her doctor and explained the dilemma. The doctor bandaged her accordingly and she headed back to the studio. As she drove through the studio gates, the watchman turned pale. People ran from everywhere to see what had happened to her. 'Davis has had a terrible accident!'

She walked quietly onto the set, and got into the hospital bed.

'You mean you're all right and this is your idea of make-up?' the director asked angrily.

'You believed it', she retorted. 'And so will the public.'

And that was the way it was photographed!

Many years ago there was a very fashionable general practitioner in London who seemed to have almost every showbusiness star as his patient. His waiting-room was very well appointed and it even had a baby grand in one corner.

On one occasion a rather elderly gentleman called to see the doctor, and after waiting for a few moments went and sat at the piano and started to play. Hardly had he struck three chords, when a very officious nurse appeared.

'You cannot play the piano', she said sharply. 'It will disturb the doctor and his patient.'

The old man apologised most profusely, and immediately closed the lid of the instrument.

'Now, what is your name?' she demanded.

'My name?' he repeated gently, 'Rachmaninoff'.

Sandy Gore is one of Australia's most talented and best known actresses. One of her best performances was in *The Legend of King O'Malley*, when she played a wonderful Australian bigot—male of course!

Things have not always been so simple for Sandy. In the production of *Halloran's Little Boat*, directed by Irene Mitchell from the now defunct St Martin's Theatre in Melbourne, Sandy had rather a difficult entrance through a trap door in the stage. It required some timing and after several attempts by Sandy to get it right, Irene became irritated. Sandy asked if she could try it just one more time.

Irene replied rather tersely, 'My dear, if we do it another fifteen times you will never get it right!'

Jon Ewing is a stage director of some note in Australia, and he also has a reputation for possessing a sabre-sharp tongue. He has been known to tear strips off actors in an unmerciful manner—but never without great provocation.

He once directed a production of *Twelve Angry Men* which he changed to *Twelve Angry Women*—with great success.

Jon has a wonderful sense of the theatrical and the end of the play was timed to music to great dramatic effect. At a given break in the music, Sheila Florence—who went on to become a household name as Lizzie Birdsworth in *Prisoner*—delivered the last line of the play, 'Not guilty'.

There had been some problems between Jon and Sheila during rehearsals and on one particular night when he was in the audience, she became so nervous that she said

'Guilty' instead of 'Not guilty', thus making nonsense of the play.

Jim Sharman's production of *King Lear* at the Melbourne Theatre Company was technically a most difficult show. Jim is also one of the most talented and unique directors in Australia today. *King Lear* is a very gruesome and violent play, and Jim didn't allow one moment to slip by unnoticed. It had everything — actresses vomiting on stage, intestines being ripped out, and people having their throats slit and their eyes gouged out. The stage was covered with blood and guts — and in the end it was all getting out of control.

Finally John Sumner said, 'The dry-cleaning bill for the audience is far too high. Either we cut some of the blood and stop spraying the people in the front row, or we issue them with plastic rain coats!'

Sir Noel Coward was staying with friends in the seaside town of Brighton in England. As he was standing on the first floor balcony looking out across the English Channel, the 8-year-old son of the family came out to join him. Looking down to the street below, he spotted two dogs in the act of making canine love. 'What are those two dogs doing?' he asked his Uncle Noel.

The master paused for a moment and then replied, 'Well you see, my dear child, the doggie in the front is blind, and the one behind is being very kind and pushing it all the way to St Dunstan's.'

Actress Anita Ekberg, who was at one time married to British film star Anthony Steel, made a film called *Zarak*. A gigantic poster of Miss Ekberg, with her fabulous body stretched from one side to the other, was placed in Leicester Square advertising the film.

The site was not supposed to be used for publicity purposes, as a building project was already in progress there. Someone pasted a sign across the most intimate part of Miss Ekberg's anatomy: THIS SITE RESERVED FOR STEEL ERECTIONS.

Investigations failed to reveal the culprit.

Barbara Cartland, the world's most prolific romantic writer, and that crusader in pink, dismissed several of her critics with a nonchalant wave of her regal hand, 'My dear', she snorted, 'Such people are motivated by two things—creative envy and smaller bank balances!'

She once drew a crowd of 5,000 people when she spoke in one of the provincial cities of England.

'If you find that your sex life is so boring that you need to swing from the chandeliers, quite clearly there is something wrong with your diet', she told her audience.

As she paused to draw breath, a young lad in the audience was heard to say, 'It just goes to show, Ma'am, that your class 'as chandeliers!'

There was a time when Miriam Karlin, star of the popular television series *The Rag Trade*, could not walk down the street without everyone calling out, 'Eh, where's your whistle?'

Even Her Majesty the Queen could not resist asking the question at one of those Royal Command performances. Just as Miriam was coming up from her curtsey, the Queen asked, 'Where's your whistle?'

Miriam looked down at her exposed cleavage and replied, 'Not on me, Ma'am!'

Australian actress Coral Browne is married to American actor Vincent Price—and very happy they are too. There are a million stories about her, most of which are unprintable. Here are three that are suitable for public consumption.

On one occasion she was at a function being held at the home of Joan and Robert Morley. She commented to Joan

Morley, as they stood observing the latest young man in Coral's life, 'You know — I am fifteen years older . . .'

'Oh come, Coral, you are much more than fifteen years older', Joan interrupted.

'I was going to say', Coral continued, 'I am fifteen years older than his mother'.

Just before she married Vincent, he agreed to re-decorate her London flat. Coral spent days hunting for the right antiques, curtains and other furnishings. At Harrods department store she found a wonderful antique bed. After she had charged it, the salesman explained there would be some delay in delivery, and that it would be a month before she could expect to have it in her flat.

'My good man', Coral announced in her most daunting tones, 'I am fifty-one years of age, and I have just taken a lover who is sixty, and I want that bed delivered tomorrow!'

Needless to add, the bed was delivered the next day.

When Coral was appearing in *The Right Honourable Gentleman* with Hugh Williams, a very pretty young man joined the company and Hugh commented to Coral that he seemed queer.

'Just because he's pretty, doesn't mean he's queer', Coral said.

'Bet you a quid', Hugh tested.

'Right', said Coral, 'I shall take him to supper after the show'.

The next night when Hugh went into Coral's dressing-room she said, 'Darling, you owe me seventeen and six!'

Rudolf Nureyev, who defected to the West years ago, brought a whole new style to the world of ballet, and in many ways he revolutionised classical dance. He does, however, enjoy a reputation for being somewhat difficult to work with.

Sir Robert Helpmann once received a telephone call at his Eaton Square home in London, asking if he would go to Paris to rehearse this new dancer Nureyev into his production of *Sleeping Beauty*. Sir Robert agreed, and left for Paris. Before he departed he was warned that although Nureyev was a brilliant dancer, he might be difficult.

Sir Robert arrived at the rehearsal room in Paris and, after watching Nureyev dance, he took him aside and spoke with him.

'I hear you can sometimes be difficult', Sir Robert said bluntly.

'Sometimes', Nureyev agreed.

'Well it is 1 o'clock, and there is a flight back to London at 3 o'clock, which I am quite happy to catch', Sir Robert said.

Nureyev was somewhat taken aback by Sir Robert's attitude, and he proved to be a delight to work with. They have since become firm friends and have worked together all over the world.

Fans sometimes say the most extraordinary things to actors, particularly when they are least expecting to see them. The late Ethel Merman always worked at a New York hospital on Wednesday afternoons when she was in town. On one occasion, wearing her pink voluntary worker's uniform, she stepped into the lift with a husband and wife team.

The wife took one look at her and said, 'Has anyone ever told you how much you look like Ethel Merman?'

Before the great star could reply the smart-alec husband butted in, 'Ethel Merman just wishes she looked like that!'

Ethel smiled sweetly, looked the man in the eye, and said, 'I *am* Ethel Merman'.

On one occasion Diana Dors was waiting at London's Heathrow Airport when a gentleman came up to her and asked, 'Aren't you Diana Dors?'

'Yes, I am', she replied.

'Well I never would have believed it', he said, turning on his heel and walking away.

There are numerous stories about the Royal Family, apocryphal or not they make for very amusing telling.

Ian 'Molly' Meldrum had the unenviable task of interviewing Prince Charles on the pop show *Countdown*. Molly was especially nervous, and when the time came to do the interview he kept blowing his lines and having to start again. With each mistake he become more nervous, until finally the Prince said, 'Why don't I interview you?'

Molly also made the fatal mistake during the pre-interview chat of saying to the Prince, 'I was in London just last week and I saw your mum at the Trooping of the Colour'.

Prince Charles, without a moment's hesitation, replied, 'You mean Her Majesty The Queen?'

The story goes that the late Princess Mary, The Princess Royal, met an acquaintance in a street in London. The man, although he could not think of the name, recognised the face. As they stood chatting he was racking his brain, but nothing would come. He asked about her family, and then she mentioned her brother.

'Oh, how is your brother?' he enquired hopefully.

'Very well', she replied.

'What is he doing these days?' he went on, searching for a lead.

'He's still the King', the Princess Royal replied sweetly.

The late Queen Mary was a regular theatregoer and rarely missed a West End show. It was customary for the cast to assemble outside the Royal Box at interval for presentation.

'I have only one complaint', Queen Mary said to Gertrude Lawrence on one of these occasions. 'I can't hear you.'

'See, what have I been telling you', Gertie said, turning to reprimand the other members of the company.

'Oh no, not them', interjected Her Majesty, 'just you!'

The Queen Mother, having just returned from a tiring engagement, called down to one of the staff at Buckingham Palace requesting an immediate gin and tonic. After a wait of sometime, she became a little impatient and ringing down again, is reported to have said, 'I don't know what you old queens are doing down there, but there is a Queen up here dying of thirst!'

Richard Todd, who was once described as Walt Disney's eighth dwarf, appeared in *The Virgin Queen* with Bette Davis. On the first day of filming he was so nervous of the great lady that he kept blowing his lines. Finally, after a number of takes, Miss Davis walked over to him and said, 'Underneath all this get-up, I'm on your side, Mr Todd'.

From that moment on things went much better!

Dame Edith Evans was one of the greatest actresses in the English-speaking world, and she was a daunting and formidable figure in the West End Theatre. Director Peter Brook once invited Dame Edith to star in a new production at the National Theatre. Brook's reputation as an avant garde director was known to Dame Edith, but she still accepted the part. However, she made it clear to Peter Brook that she wanted no part of his modern theories on acting. According to the great lady there was only one way to get it right—constant rehearsal.

For two weeks the cast sat around discussing the play, the thought processes, and all those things which actors want to worry about. Dame Edith found it most interesting but felt it had nothing to do with the theatre, and absolutely nothing to do with acting. Finally, unable to contain herself any longer, she said, 'Mr Brook, young man! When are we going to start rehearsal? I don't have long to live!'

Dame Gladys Moncrieff (Our Glad) had a favourite press cutting headline. When she was appearing in *Maid of the Mountains* and *Rio Rita* with John McCallum, she had just recovered from a broken leg she had sustained in a car accident. On leaving hospital she was sent masses of flowers, in particular orchids, which she loved.

She pinned as many as she could onto her clothes, and the rest she managed to attach to the single crutch she was forced to use. The local newspaper carried the headline: DAME GLADYS LEAVES HOSPITAL WITH ORCHIDS PINNED ALL OVER HER CRUTCH!

Everybody remembers Jack Benny and the constant references to his meanness. John McCallum, who brought him to Australia for a highly successful tour, testifies to that meanness and recalls that it was a characteristic he shared with Maurice Chevalier. When he came to Australia John and Googie, both of whom are most generous hosts, extended the full Australian hospitality, which takes some beating. They wined and dined him, and took him absolutely everywhere. When he left Chevalier presented Googie with a 2s. bunch of violets!

One of Jacki Weaver's first television appearances was in the Crawford series *Animal Doctor*. The storyline involved a tiger which was suffering from toothache and Jacki's character had to track it down and take care of the problem.

On the day of shooting everybody except Jacki and the assistant keeper were in huge cages. The assistant keeper, a callow, pimply-faced youth, was armed with a whip and a rifle and kept assuring Jacki that the head keeper would arrive at any moment.

In the course of the action Jacki had to feed the tiger ice cream cones which were actually filled with fillet steak. The animal was not especially friendly and kept snapping at Jacki, almost removing her hand on several occasions.

Finally, after she had been filming for about two hours, the callow youth smiled with relief as a car pulled up on the location. 'The keeper's arrived', he announced to Jacki.

As the man got out of the car, Jacki could hardly believe her eyes—he had only one arm!

When she was studying to be an actress Jacki supplemented her income by singing on various television shows, including *Bandstand*. One of the record companies decided to turn her into a pop star and she released a record called 'Something's Got a Hold on Me', with 'Raining in My Heart' on the flip side. It sold only 159 copies!

However, she made up for it years later when she received a gold album for the cast recording of *Playing Our Song* with John Waters.

When a young lady asked Zsa Zsa Gabor what she should do with her ring after a broken engagement Zsa Zsa replied, 'Darlink, you should give back ze ring but keep ze stone!'

Asked how she came to have such a fabulous collection of jewellery Zsa Zsa quipped, 'Darlink, I never hated a man so much I gave him back his diamonds'.

It is not true that Zsa Zsa once said, 'I am a wonderful housekeeper. Whenever I get a divorce I get to keep the house!'

When asked about the 'quote', she replied, 'No, it is so famous I only wish I had said it!'

The line actually came from a comedian who was appearing in Las Vegas.

Following on the success of *The Elocution of Benjamin Franklin* in both London and New York, Gordon Chater obtained a green card and eventually permanent alien residency of America, and he has settled now in New York. When he returned to Australia to appear in the stage play *The Dresser* with Warren Mitchell, he was questioned a number of times about why he was living in New York instead of Australia.

For the first half dozen times, Gordon attempted to explain the reasons. Finally, he became so bored with the question that he answered rather tersely, 'Why do I live in New York? Because the milk is cheaper!'

Australian Helen Montague is one of the most successful theatrical producers in London's West End. She is also a great supporter of Australian talent. One year, Helen took a David Williamson play to London, and Qantas agreed to fly the artists there on a contra arrangement. The deal stipulated that a sign reading 'Fly Qantas' would be posted outside the theatre.

Just as the sign was about to be put into place, it occurred to Helen that it was not such a good idea. She asked the workmen to wait while she went into the theatre to phone Qantas.

'I really don't think it is such a good idea', she said to the Qantas spokesman.

'Why?' he asked.

'Well, it looks rather odd beside the name of the play, which is *What If You Died Tomorrow*.'

After his bankruptcy trial in London's famous Old Bailey, Wilfred Hyde-Whyte was met by the press as he left the court. They asked him how it had felt in the courtroom.

Obviously relieved it was all over, Hyde-Whyte answered, 'Very quiet, a bit like a bad Wednesday Matinee in Shaftsbury Avenue'.

It was midnight when Marlene Dietrich arrived at London airport, having flown from Paris where Christian Dior had just completed the wardrobe for her latest film, *Stage Fright*.

Miss Dietrich was tired and unsmiling when she entered the lounge to meet the waiting press. When one of the photographers asked her to raise her skirt to show a little more of the famous legs, she smiled her famous ambiguous smile and said, 'If it's true that my legs are my fortune, why should I show them to you for nothing?'

She raised her skirt no more than one inch while the photographers clicked away!

As part of the publicity for *Stage Fright*, Marlene had agreed to a lengthy photographic session with Picturepost. Although the results were stunning, the editorial staff felt there might be another angle which they had not explored. It was agreed they could meet with Miss Dietrich for five minutes to discuss further possibilities.

Dietrich received them in a private suite below the River Room in London's Savoy. Unfortunately she was not in a particularly accommodating mood.

'Miss Dietrich, the pictures we have are wonderful but we feel there might be something you could suggest which would extend the story — another angle which we may have overlooked.'

'Such as?' she enquired.

'Frankly, we are not quite sure. We thought we might photograph you at the races, or a society ball.'

'Go on', she said, unmoved by their dilemma.

'Well, Miss Dietrich, we might suggest your being photographed in Bond Street, or one of the more fashionable night spots in London.'

'You might suggest that', she said unsmilingly.

'Miss Dietrich, is there anything you have not been photographed doing?' they asked in desperation.

'Yes', she replied after a moment's hesitation.

No further photographs were taken, however, and the feature appeared as it was originally planned.

During the days of *The Mavis Bramston Show*, Gordon Chater lived at White Beach in Sydney. Among his show business neighbours were Googie Withers and John McCallum.

Googie is famous for her Sunday luncheons and on one occasion Gordon arrived to be greeted at the front door by Googie, who said in her inimitable tone, 'Darling, the house is full of people who love us, and never pay to see us!'

Sir Noel Coward is famous for his one-liners, which invariably left people flabbergasted. He once said, 'Television is for appearing on — not watching!'

Of writers he said, 'We in the industry know that behind every successful screen writer stands a woman — and behind her — his wife'.

During the Coronation procession in 1953, Queen Salote of Tonga rode in an open carriage and, despite the constant drizzle, she would not allow the hood to be raised, much to the delight of the crowd.

Sir Noel Coward was watching the procession on television with a group of friends. When the cameras picked up Queen Salote someone asked who the gentleman was riding with the Queen of Tonga.

'Her lunch', replied Sir Noel.

Claudette Colbert was having trouble with her lines and said to the Master. 'Darling, I'm so sorry. I knew them backwards last night.'

'And that is exactly how you are saying them this morning', he snapped.

When a young actor insisted on questioning Sir Noel about his motivation for a particular line, the Master became impatient and replied, 'Your motivation, my dear boy, is your cheque on Thursday'.

To another young man he said, 'Don't look at the floor, there is nothing down there except your performance!'

One of the most famous Sir Noel Coward comments, which has become a catch phrase in the theatre, goes something like this. During rehearsals a young and rather over enthusiastic actor was driving Sir Noel mad with questions about his very small part.

'What do you want me to do in this scene?' he asked the Master.

'Just say your words, and don't bump into the furniture', Sir Noel replied.

Frank Thring, Googie Withers and John McCallum were appearing together in the stage play *The Kingfisher*. It was an especially hot January in Melbourne and the heat, coupled with the rather small houses, were testing tempers to the limit. Frank and Googie had several minor contretemps, and although they are the very best of friends, relationships became a little strained at times.

Frank had taken to wearing a rather large bauble around his neck and his constant references to the adornment as a 'diamond' were beginning to rankle with Googie. Finally, unable to contain herself any longer, she turned on him and said rather sharply, 'Oh come on, darling, if that were a diamond it would be in the Queen's collection'.

'Well isn't it?' said Frank without missing a beat.

During one season, the Chichester Festival Theatre—one of England's most prestigious company of actors—was performing *A Woman Of No Importance*. Sian Phillips was the star, and she was supported by Ambrosine Phillpotts,

Margaretta Scott (*All Creatures Great and Small*) and Barbara Murray.

The three ladies had only been onstage for a few minutes when an American tourist shouted in a very abusive voice, 'Speak up, I can't hear you!'

The ladies were stunned. They looked at each other, there was a quick exchange between them, then they rose from their chairs, curtsied to the audience, left the stage and came back and started the scene all over again.

Needless to say, the whole thing was done to a great round of applause from the audience.

Gordon Chater has a reputation for insisting that all props and sound effects be at the rehearsal ten days before a show opens. On one occasion he was having problems with the technical crew, and he felt time was running out.

'She'll be right', he was told. 'It'll all be there in Melbourne for you.'

'In time for the opening night — or after?' Gordon snapped back.

Rex Harrison met his long time friend Robert Morley in the Burlington Arcade in London.

'You know, Robert', Rex said, 'I really do envy you. For the last fifty years you've had the same wife, the same house and, if I might say so, the same performance!'

Publicist Patti Mostyn telephoned one of the wire services to confirm the press conference arrangements for an international artist she was looking after in Australia. After giving the date, time, location, and name of the artist, she asked the operator to repeat the details.

'Press conference tomorrow, 6th May, 10.30 a.m., The Hilton Hotel, Little Archie', he read back to her.

'No', said Patti in disbelief. 'Not Little Archie — Liberace!'

Dame Gladys Cooper, the mother-in-law of Robert Morley and grandmother of the Australian-based theatrical producer Wilton Morley, was one of the great beauties of her time. She was also one of the most colourful personalities of the British Theatre.

On one occasion Dame Gladys swept into a restaurant—she never entered, she always swept in—only to be told the restaurant was totally booked out by General Motors.

'Oh, General Motors', she exclaimed. 'He is an old friend of mine—I'm sure you can squeeze me in somewhere!'

The Australian press have, in the past, enjoyed a reputation overseas for asking rather extraordinary questions. It seems chiefs of staff feel that performers—no matter how famous—are there for the benefit of cadet reports to practise their interviewing technique. Stars have been stopped dead in their tracks by some of the questions.

'How does it feel to be a has-been?' one young reporter asked Rock Hudson.

'I don't know', he replied without missing a beat, 'I've never been one!'

'Tell me Miss Leigh, did you have a very big part in *Gone With The Wind?*' What the lady replied is unprintable, but the young man certainly got the message!

'Is it true, Sir Thomas, that you are related to the famous Beecham pills?'

'Yes', he replied, 'and I hope my music moves you as much!'

Critics—whom Frank Thring once described as being like 'pianists in a brothel, always managing to get between the customer and the goods'—can be the kiss of death if they pan a show.

There have been some extraordinary reviews for performances over the years. One of the notices for the production of *Richard III* at the Community Theatre in Sydney went something like this:

'Alexander Archdale's production of *Richard III* at the Community Theatre, with Peter Adams in the title role, has all the possibilities of being a very good radio play, except the voices aren't good enough!'

Film actor Richard Todd is best remembered for his screen performance in *A Man Called Peter*, but he also appeared in a number of stage roles, including Oscar Wilde's *An Ideal Husband*. He carried around with him a copy of one review which even he, with his limited sense of humour, found amusing. It read: 'Richard Todd in the role of Lord Goring, delivered Oscar Wilde's epigrams like a fishwife throwing dead mackerel on a marble slab!'

Jennifer Hagan and Frederick Parslow were appearing in a Melbourne Theatre Company production of *Much Ado About Nothing*, directed by John Sumner, with costume designs by Kristian Fredrikson. There is little doubt that Jennifer and Fred qualified as the best looking Beatrice and Benedick ever to appear on the Australian stage.

The production, after its Melbourne season, went on a Victorian country tour. John Sumner paid a visit to the Company in one of the towns to see how the playing was standing up to the rigours of touring. During the note session which followed, he mentioned one particular scene to Jennifer and Fred. 'I go away leaving a perfectly nice little love scene, and I come back and what do I find? Two people sitting on a bench shouting at each other!'

Melbourne Theatre Company actors have always had a reputation for very loud delivery, mostly because John Sumner is partially deaf, and he spends half his life saying, 'I can't hear you!'

Veteran actor Maurie Fields once said of another actor, 'What he knows about acting you could write on a pinhead with a six-inch nail!'

Dame Nellie Melba is alleged to have advised a contemporary who was planning a concert tour of the Antipodes, 'Give 'em muck—it's all they understand'.

When Pamela Stevenson was invited to launch the first Half Tix Booth (two theatre tickets for the price of one on the day of the performance) in Victoria, she very cleverly turned the quote to suit her ends.

'Nellie Melba said give 'em muck', she told a packed audience at the Rockman's Regency Hotel in Melbourne, 'but even this great lady didn't have the wisdom or the foresight to give 'em muck at half price!'